Speaking God's Words

This book is dedicated
to my fellow workers in gospel ministry
in Melbourne and Victoria

Speaking God's Words

A practical theology of preaching

Peter Adam

Vicar of St Jude's, Carlton,
Melbourne, Australia

The 1993 Moore College Lectures

Inter-Varsity Press

INTER-VARSITY PRESS
38 De Montfort Street, Leicester LE1 7GP, England

© Peter Adam 1996

First published 1996
Reprinted 1996

British Library Cataloguing in Publication Data
A catalogue record for this book is available from the British Library.

ISBN 0-85111-171-8

Set in Ehrhardt
Typeset in Great Britain by Parker Typesetting Service, Leicester
Printed in Great Britain by Clays Ltd, St Ives plc

Inter-Varsity Press is the book-publishing division of the Universities and Colleges Christian Fellowship (formerly the Inter-Varsity Fellowship), a student movement linking Christian Unions in universities and colleges throughout the United Kingdom and the Republic of Ireland, and a member movement of the International Fellowship of Evangelical Students. For information about local and national activities write to UCCF, 38 De Montfort Street, Leicester LE1 7GP.

Contents

Foreword

I am an enthusiast for this book. Much of its substance I first heard, in lecture form, at a conference for young ministers of the gospel. What I recall is the startling freshness of what Dr Peter Adam was saying. I remember the initial minutes when polite attention, as well as a certain sleepiness after long journeys, changed to a growing delight and expectancy. Minds began to focus. Here was an instructor who had thought deeply as a consequence of extensive reading and long practical experience. The distinctive humour, very dry, also helped. So did modest claims and mastery of material. We knew, I think, that others would have to enjoy this radical tuition. So you will understand why I am glad that those lectures, developed in many similar situations, are now available in permanent form.

The numerous quotations, from giants such as Calvin and Baxter, as well as from fine modern writers, are a feature of *Speaking God's Words*. There are gems here. It would take most of us many moons to assemble a similar treasury of wisdom. But for me they are not the heart of this book, which is to be found in Dr Adam's own perspectives and judgments.

He is notably good, for example, on the necessary foundations for Christian preaching. These occupy all of Part 1, and should not be skipped by those eager for the practical help promised by the author in his introduction, and duly delivered in later chapters. I write this foreword in a week when, in London, a new prize is being awarded for the Preacher of the Year. The appointment of an atheist as one of the adjudicators, while pleasing to satirists and other collectors of representative modern absurdities, suggests a massive misunderstanding on the part of the organizers as to what constitutes Christian preaching. If exceptional communication skills are a main desideratum, then the 'super-apostles' of Corinth, and their many disciples, would walk away with the prizes in a similar first-century contest. They would see no reason to fear a threat to their supremacy from the great apostle (in view of their sour verdict on him, given in 2 Cor. 10:10). As for Paul, his expectations were undoubtedly of a prize, but a heavenly one; in this world he knew he was much more likely to be awarded a prison sentence for his bold testimony to Christ.

The demise of true Christian preaching in the wider church of the twentieth century is attributable directly to the doubts distilled by much modern theology for successive generations of ministerial students. The

7

familiar explanations for empty pews, such as modern minds, modern materialism, and the modern media, are quite unconvincing. When we ask whether there is still a spiritual hunger in the land there can be only one answer; and when we ask whether there has been, particularly in the twentieth century, a famine of the Word of the Lord in our land, again there is only one honest reply. The bread of life has been scarce, but when it is available in generous measure, queues to possess it are not unknown. However, the situation in the whole church community can change for the better only when we are convinced again that 'God has spoken', that his Word 'is written', and that 'Preach the Word' is the one absolute and definitive command laid on the people of God. Then we might again 'fill Jerusalem' with our teaching (*cf.* Acts 5:28). In going back to such basic principles as these Peter Adam has my gratitude.

Then I particularly welcome section 1 of chapter 4, in which our author, though himself given to an effective pulpit ministry, explains that the teaching of the Word of God in the congregation is wider than pulpit work, indispensable as that must always be. In seeking to restore the preaching ministry to its proper place, we have no grounds for silencing all the other teaching ministries that characterize a living church or Christian family. This reminder was much commented on at the conference to which I have referred; it remains a useful balancing perspective.

Another thoughtful chapter, 5, invites us to look at the preacher's Bible and see the relationship between it and his preaching (we must assume that there is one). Eight key issues, frequently discussed, such as the *effectiveness*, *nature* and *relevance* of Scripture, are dealt with wisely and well.

By now I trust that any bookstall browsers, following me thus far, will have had their appetites whetted to possess this excellent training manual for aspiring and active preachers, and will be impatient to begin their study of it. Truly the author's aim, that this should be a robust practical theology of preaching, has been achieved. I particularly like that word 'robust', for this quality, rightly understood, should be an ingredient in all powerful preaching. According to my thesaurus the reverse of 'robust' is 'mealy-mouthed, unhealthy, unrealistic, and weak'. May we be delivered from all such preaching, rightly despised by our unchurched neighbours in their thousands. And may this book play its part in the encouragement of Christian preachers everywhere for the great work ahead of them.

Dick Lucas
St Helen's Church,
Bishopsgate, London

Preface

My aim in this book is to provide a robust practical theology of preaching as part of the ministry of the Word in the local congregation. I want to provide a *theology* of preaching, because only theological arguments are convincing in the long term. To argue that we ought to preach because it works, or that we ought not to preach because preaching is ineffective, is to descend to the realm of the merely pragmatic. And to go on preaching without substantial reformation and renewal of our practice of preaching is to minister without imagination or faith. 'The practical man merely repeats the mistakes of his predecessors,' wrote Disraeli. And that is certainly true in the area of Christian ministry. We also need a theology of preaching, because the practice of preaching suffers nowadays from an uncertain theological base. Changes over recent years in our theology of God's revelation, of the Bible, of Christian formation, of communication, of community and of ecclesiology have tended to undermine preaching. In such a situation it is not wise to continue a ministry without a deep conviction about its sound theological base.

We also need a *robust* theology of preaching because the general mood of our church life and world is against preaching, and even a convinced preacher can easily grow disheartened and either give up on preparation for preaching, or else continue the activity but without much expectation of results. We need a *robust* theology of preaching, too, not only because the intellectual and theological climate of our age is opposed to preaching, but also because preaching is such a demanding activity. I am never sure whether it is the preparation or the presentation which is more demanding! And all the pressure on a pastor or minister is to spend time and creative energy being a counsellor, social worker, administrator, friendly visitor or public-relations worker. The pastor needs a robust theology of preaching to find any time or energy for preparation, let alone to find time to preach during a service or meeting which is already full of singing, notices, prayers and 'fellowship time'.

We also need a *practical* theology of preaching. I have been greatly helped by reading Sidney Greidanus's *The Modern Preacher and the Ancient Text*;[1] I wish I had read it years ago. Its perspective is that of the lecture-room in the seminary, college or university, so I shall attempt to provide a complementary perspective, that of the pulpit and minister's study. It is preaching as part of the pastoral ministry that is my concern. I hope that I can be *practical* in at least four ways: by showing again that the

Bible is practical in its teaching on the ministry of the Word, by illustrating various helpful models of ministry from the history of the Christian churches, by giving examples from my own ministry, and by including some practical advice.

I began preaching as a student at St Thomas', South Richmond, a small building in a light-industrial area of Melbourne, with a congregation of five or six elderly people. It was a great place to start – and a very forgiving congregation. In London I preached for two years at St George the Martyr, Queen Square. It had a perfect acoustic for preaching and a small congregation. But it was a most engaging group to preach for. It was their custom to discuss the sermon for half an hour over coffee after the service. It was great to get that feedback, and good to get stimulation to try new ways of preaching. My time in Durham included a wide range of preaching and teaching, from congregations of tertiary students, to the compulsory chapel at the Remand Centre at Low Newton, to the essentially Church of England experience of St Cuthbert's, Durham, and St Aidan's, Framwellgate Moor, and in various chapels of the University colleges.

For the last fourteen years I have preached at the increasingly diverse congregations of St Jude's, Carlton, back in Melbourne. What a privilege to have a people who are happy to work through Hebrews together over nine months! And how rewarding to preach through 1 Corinthians in a (then unheated) barn of a building, and see congregations growing and maturing by God's power! Through the weekly discipline of preparing and preaching, many have come to faith in Christ and to maturity in life, many have been equipped in ministry and challenged to significant Christian ministries, and our congregations have been built up to maturity in Christ. All this has happened as God has used the prayer, ministry, generosity and love of many people, but it has been a great joy to me to see in all of this the ways in which God has directly and unmistakably used the preaching of his Word.

I have written this book with the following questions in mind. What does the Bible teach us about the ministry of the Word? What are the current questions about preaching? What can I say that will have theological substance and be of practical usefulness to those who preach? My aim is to argue, expand and illustrate the following points.

1. The role and priority of preaching as part of the ministry of the Word.

2. The need for the Bible to determine the content and style of our preaching.

3. What preaching will and will not achieve.

4. The need of the three elements of exegesis, application and exhortation within preaching.

5. The role of the sermon in modelling and teaching responsible and theological use of the Bible and application to modern life.

6. How we can learn from models of ministry and preaching of former generations of believers.

7. The need for the preacher to love and serve the congregation.

8. The role of preaching in producing conversions to Christ, and both individual and corporate maturity in faith.

In Part 1, we lay down three biblical foundations of preaching. These are meant to provide a firm theological basis for what follows, and, more significantly, to provide us with great confidence in God's call to our ministry. In Part 2, we look at the preacher at work: at preaching as a ministry of the Word, the preacher's use of the Bible, the purpose of the preacher, and the demands of preaching.

I am grateful to the Revd Dr Peter Jensen, Principal of Moore Theological College, Sydney, for inviting me to give the Moore College Lectures in 1993. These lectures form the basis of this book. I began my preparation for these lectures by reading through the Bible with the question, 'What does the Bible teach us about the ministry of the Word, and especially about preaching?' I have re-used and reworked this material with groups of clergy in Armidale (NSW), in Melbourne, at Ridley College and in my Timothy Institute Preachers' Workshops, and in Britain under the auspices of the Proclamation Trust.

I am very grateful to the Vestry and people of St Jude's, Carlton, for allowing me time to prepare and give these lectures, and to prepare them for publication. I write as a pastor, and the writing of this book has been done in the midst of church duties. I am very grateful to Janis Lampard for her meticulous work in deciphering and typing.

Notes

1. Sidney Greidanus, *The Modern Preacher and the Ancient Text* (Grand Rapids: Eerdmans; Leicester: IVP, 1988).

Part 1

Three biblical foundations of preaching

1

God has spoken

In order to provide a robust practical theology of preaching, we shall need to dig wide and deep to lay some foundations. In this chapter we shall dig *wide*, in that our subject will be the ministry of the Word which, as we shall see, is a wider subject than preaching. The ministry of the Word in the Bible includes the writing and reading of Scripture, and the use of Scripture in personal exhortation and encouragement as well as in public teaching and preaching. Preaching is best understood as one part of the ministry of the Word, and it derives its theological character from the biblical basis for all aspects of the ministry of the Word. So later we shall dig *deep*, in trying to establish the great theological foundations of all ministries of the Word, including preaching and teaching.

In this chapter we look at the first of three great theological foundations of preaching: the belief that *God has spoken*, that his words remain powerful, and that without this historic revelation of God in words there can be no ministry of the Word. The basis for any true human speaking for God is that God is a speaking God. Any human ministry of the Word depends on a God who is not silent. If God is dumb, then we may have a ministry of words, but not of the Word, God's Word. And it is clear that the God of the Bible is a God who speaks.

God's words in the Bible

God's revelation begins with a sermon; God preaches and the world is made. 'God said, "Let there be light", and there was light.' Six sermons are preached in a wonderful sequence; the Word of God is proclaimed in heaven's pulpit and all comes to pass; the preaching forms the universe . . . the Word preached is no empty word; it accomplishes what it pleases and never returns void to him who speaks.[1]

God speaks, and his words are powerful, effective and creative of reality. The God who *speaks* is the God who *acts* through his words.

All the different forms of Old Testament literature reflect and convey the words of God: without God speaking there could be no promise, no covenant, no law, no story, no prophecy, no wise saying, no apocalyptic. The literary forms of the New Testament also reflect and convey the words of God through gospel, parable, letter, and prophecy. It seems obvious that the God who 'spoke, and it came to be' (Ps. 33:9) in creation, the God who spoke at Sinai, who spoke 'in many and various ways by the prophets', has spoken too by his Son (Heb. 1:1–2).

The evidence for the idea that God speaks is found not only in those instances where the text of the Bible describes God speaking, and records God's words. It is also found in the Bible's polemic against idolatry, in its teaching on humankind made in God's image, and in the incarnation. In Psalm 115 the argument is that idolatry is futile because of the impotence of idols, in contrast to the God of Israel.

> Our God is in the heavens;
>   he does whatever he pleases.
> Their idols are silver and gold,
>   the work of human hands.
> They have mouths, but do not speak;
>   eyes, but do not see.
> They have ears, but do not hear;
>   noses, but do not smell.
> They have hands, but do not feel,
>   feet, but do not walk;
>   they make no sound in their throats.
> Those who make them are like them;
>   so are all who trust in them.
>
> (Ps. 115:3–8)

Or again in the court case in Isaiah 41, the strongest contrast is drawn between the idols who cannot speak or predict, and the LORD God who acts and speaks.

> Set forth your case, says the LORD;
>   bring your proofs, says the King of Jacob.
> Let them bring them, and tell us what is to happen.
> Tell us the former things, what they are,
>   so that we may consider them,
> and that we may know their outcome;
>   or declare to us the things to come.
> Tell us what is to come hereafter,
>   that we may know that you are gods;
> do good, or do harm,
>   that we may be afraid and terrified . . .

Who declared it from the beginning, so that we might know,
    and beforehand, so that we might say, 'He is right'?
There was no one who declared it, none who proclaimed,
    none who heard your words.
I first have declared it to Zion
    and I give to Jerusalem a herald of good tidings.
But when I look there is no one;
    among these there is no counsellor
    who, when I ask, gives an answer.

(Is. 41:21–23, 25–28)

Again, the Bible's teaching on humankind made in God's image assumes a God who speaks. In Genesis 1, as we have seen, God speaks. 'Let there be light' (3); 'Let there be a dome in the midst of the waters' (6); 'let the dry ground appear' (9); 'Let there be lights . . .' (14). It is this speaking God who then says, 'Let us make humankind in our image, according to our likeness' (1:26). And the creation of male and female is immediately followed by the words that God speaks to them, 'Be fruitful and multiply . . . I have given you every plant yielding seed . . .' (1:28–29). In Genesis 2 the creation of the man is followed by the command: 'You may freely eat of every tree of the garden; but of the tree of the knowledge of good and evil you shall not eat, for in the day that you eat of it you shall die' (2:16–17). Later the man speaks: 'This at last is bone of my bones . . .' (2:23). God, the speaking God, makes humans in his own image and speaks to them. Our speech and hearing are a sign that God speaks and hears (Ps. 94:9–10).

The doctrine of the incarnation assumes that God is a speaking God. If we take the view that God is essentially dumb, then the words of Jesus become merely human, the product of his humanity and not of his divinity. But when Jesus uses the double Amen as a preface to his statements (*e.g.* Jn. 6:26, 32, 47, 53), he is claiming to speak as God. The words of Jesus reflect the God who speaks, and Jesus also forms his life in obedience to the words of God. 'One does not live by bread alone, but by every word that comes from the mouth of God' (Mt. 4:4). His frequent use of the formula 'it is written' demonstrates his commitment to the words of God (*e.g.* Mt. 4:4, 6, 7, 10). Jesus also says that he receives his teaching from the Father, that those who belong to God hear what God says, and that he has given his disciples the words given him by the Father (Jn. 7:16; 8:47; 17:8).

The Bible's teaching on idolatry, the image of God, and the incarnation, then, further illustrates the doctrine of the God who speaks.

Objections: Temple and Dulles

Despite this overwhelming evidence, modern theology has an aversion to the words of God, and to the idea that God speaks. For many modern writers, God's revelation is a revelation of his person: 'All revelation is the self-revelation of God.'[2] In the often-quoted words of William Temple, 'What is offered to man's apprehension in any specific revelation is not truth concerning God but the living God himself.'[3] Our modern thinking may allow that God is, that he engages in self-disclosure, that he acts, that he gives signs of his presence, or that he appears in visions, but it is curiously coy about the belief that he speaks.

My argument is that this viewpoint separates what is seen as being together in Scripture. I am not arguing that speaking is the only form of revelation; but in the Bible the God who is present to act, to give signs of his presence, and to disclose himself, is also the God who speaks. Take, for example, the revelation of God at Mount Sinai. God has come down to rescue his people from the hand of the Egyptians (Ex. 3:8), and now descends to the top of Mount Sinai (Ex. 19:20). God is present. While the people may not see God, Moses and the elders see the God of Israel (Ex. 19:21; 24:10). God is seen. There are visible signs of his presence: thunder and lightning, thick cloud, trumpet blast, smoke and fire (Ex. 19:16–19). All these are part of the revelation, but it is obvious that the main content of the revelation comes in words; it is by God's words that Moses knows to come near, and by God's speaking that the Ten Words are given and the covenant explained. The words of God are not only spoken but written down, and the name and glory of God are revealed in the word proclaimed by the LORD as he passes by Moses. 'The LORD, the LORD, a God merciful and gracious . . .' (Ex. 19:20–24; 34:5–6).

When Temple distinguishes between the 'truth concerning God' and 'the living God himself', he is the victim and perpetrator of a false dichotomy. The God who is present is the God who speaks. If Exodus is about the presence of Yahweh,[4] it also conveys the words of Yahweh, including the crucial words of the covenant.

The Bible's assumption is that part of God's self-revelation includes his speaking, and that the Bible contains the words of God, for example in his promise to Abram, and his words from Mount Sinai. I am not here addressing the more difficult question of how the parts of the Bible that do not come in the form of words from God can rightly be described as the words or Word of God. I also recognize that some books of the Bible, for example Esther and Proverbs, make no reference to the words of God as God speaking. But I take it that by a process of extension those parts of the Old Testament that are not in the form of 'words from God' come to be recognized as God's words. Thus Jesus quotes Genesis 2:24 as authoritative in his discussion about divorce and marriage, though in

Genesis 2 these words are part of the narrative, not the quoted words of God.

The current objection to the notion of a speaking God lies deep in the heart of much modern theology. For example, Avery Dulles, in his *Models of Revelation*,[5] surveys five models of revelation: revelation as doctrine, as history, as inner experience, as dialectical presence, and as new awareness. The notion of God speaking is found most clearly in models 1 and 4. But in his study of model 1, on revelation as doctrine, he makes four assumptions which severely affect his treatment of these ideas.

First, he defines revelation as doctrine solely in terms of propositional revelation. While many of those who write in support of the idea of God speaking assume that propositional revelation is co-extensive with the idea of God speaking, this is not the case. In the Bible the revelation recorded certainly includes propositional statements, such as 'The LORD, the LORD, a God merciful and gracious . . .' (Ex. 34:6), 'I am the God of your father, the God of Abraham, the God of Isaac, and the God of Jacob' (Ex. 3:6), 'I am the good shepherd' (Jn. 10:11), 'I have no pleasure in the death of anyone, says the LORD God' (Ezk. 18:32). And because a propositional statement affirms or denies something,[6] propositional revelation is the form of revelation in which the content is clear and brief. Although biblical revelation includes propositions, however, it also includes many other forms of revelation, such as stories, parables and descriptions of the temple. A biblical doctrine of God's words will certainly include the idea of propositional revelation, but needs to include other categories of revelation as well. (This has important implications for preaching, which I will describe later; chapter 4.)

Dulles thus accepts a limited notion of revelation which he seems to have taken from writers about Scripture rather than from Scripture itself.

Secondly, Dulles assumes that an acceptance of the notion of revelation as doctrine precludes the acceptance of revelation as history or divine presence. Perhaps he falls into this error because of the structure of his study of revelation. This is a common error in modern writing on revelation, and a very unhelpful one, as we have already seen. For, as we saw in Exodus 19, the God who was present, who was working in history, and who showed signs of his presence, was also the God who spoke.

Thirdly, Dulles defines the response called for by the concept of propositional revelation as 'assent'. The language of 'assent to doctrine' is intended to underline the merely cerebral, dry and scholastic nature of this model of revelation. Dulles is quite wrong. The response called for in the Bible to the hearing of the words of God is not mere assent, but faith in God who speaks the promise, obedience to the God who commands, faithfulness to the God who has made his covenant plain, return to the God who warns, and hope in the God who foretells the future. To respond to God's words is to respond to *God*: God is present in the speaking of his words.

Dulles also assumes that the statement of doctrine is a powerless exercise, whereas 'the word of God is living and active . . . piercing until it divides soul from spirit, joints from marrow' (Heb. 4:12). The coming of the word of God brings new birth (1 Pet. 1:23). Indeed,

> The law of the LORD is perfect,
>   reviving the soul;
> the decrees of the LORD are sure,
>   making wise the simple;
> the precepts of the LORD are right,
>   rejoicing the heart;
> the commandment of the LORD is clear,
>   enlightening the eyes;
> the fear of the LORD is pure,
>   enduring for ever;
> the ordinances of the LORD are true
>   and righteous altogether.
> More to be desired are they than gold,
>   even much fine gold;
> sweeter also than honey,
>   and drippings from the honeycomb.
>
> Moreover by them is your servant warned;
>   in keeping them there is great reward.
>
> (Ps. 19:7–11)

Dulles's notion of 'assent to doctrine' is thus an entirely inadequate description of the power of the Word of God, and of the effect and total response to the living God that it produces.

Paul Helm's comment on the anti-propositional stance of Dulles and others is apt:

> It is a curious and interesting historical fact that while the idea that the Bible is God's special propositional revelation has been charged with replacing God himself by propositions about God, an examination of the literature during periods when such a view was dominant suggests the exact reverse. In the first Chapter of the *Westminster Confession of Faith* (often said to be the product of what is regarded as theological decadence, 'Reformed Scholasticism'), we are told that 'it pleased the Lord, at sundry times, and in diverse manners, *to reveal himself*'. And in the *Westminster Shorter Catechism*, Question

20

86, 'What is faith in Jesus Christ?' is answered as follows: 'Faith in Jesus Christ is a saving grace, whereby we receive and rest upon him alone for salvation, as he is offered to us in the gospel.' In the eyes of the Westminster Divines at least the words and propositions of the gospel are not a barrier to faith in Christ, they are a necessary condition of that faith.[7]

Fourthly, the examples that Dulles offers of this model of revelation as doctrine are those of conservative evangelicalism and scholastic Roman Catholicism of the last 100 years. In this way he gives the impression that this is a recent view of revelation, a by-product of various forces and movements within our society. As Bruce Vawter has shown, however, the notion that revelation includes verbal content has had a long history in the thought of the Christian church, and indeed was assumed to be true until fairly recently.[8] From Catholics to Quakers, all have assumed that revelation comes in words.[9] And as we have seen, this is not an unreasonable assumption, given the biblical description of the God who speaks.

There may be many explanations why modern theology has moved away from the idea of the speaking God, and has attempted to displace it by separating it from other models of revelation, identifying these models as primary (God as present, the God who acts), and then forcing a false dichotomy between these true models and the rejected model of the God who speaks. I suspect that reasons for this move include a desire to preserve the transcendence of God, and a belief that words are too feeble a vehicle adequately to convey more than a poor reflection of divine truth. But is God so transcendent that he cannot use words such as humans use? Is he so mysterious, so 'other' or so secretive that he cannot or will not reveal anything about himself or any aspect of his will, and that there cannot be any content to any revelation? Is God too transcendent to speak? If God used words that humans use, would that compromise his transcendence? Are human words too feeble to convey any part of divine truth?

The answer to all these questions is *no*. God's transcendence is not such that it reduces his power and ability to communicate. To say that God is so transcendent that he cannot use words that are comprehensible to human beings is to adopt a false view of transcendence. For transcendence is not at the cost of God's involvement and interaction with the universe he created; that would be a deistic transcendence. Theistic, biblical transcendence means that the sovereign God is totally free to be involved in the intimate detail of his creation without compromising his transcendence. The sovereign transcendence of God means he can be immanent within his universe, act within it, and communicate within it, without losing his transcendent power. His immanence within the world and revelation expresses his transcendence. The biblical assumption is not only that God may use human words to reveal himself, but that he has done so. Revelation that is presence or act or sign, without verbal interpretation, is incomplete.

God speaks. What does this mean?

At this point we need to define a little more clearly what we mean by the phrases 'the God who speaks', and 'the words of God'. A common understanding of these phrases is that they are anthropomorphisms, employing human words or characteristics to describe God. To use the language of 'speaking' with respect to God is to use the best way we have of describing what is happening, even if God does not speak physically.

It is interesting to notice that adherents of various theological systems select the areas in which they detect the presence of anthropomorphisms. For some, it is language about God's presence; for others, God's actions; for others, God's emotions; for others, God's speaking; while for others, any language about God is anthropomorphic.

What happens when God communicates with human beings? The most natural assumption in Genesis 12 is that when God spoke, audible sounds were heard. 'The LORD had said to Abram, "Go from your country and your kindred and your father's house to the land that I will show you"' (Gn. 12:1). Certainly on the great day on Mount Sinai, the sound of God's voice was heard, and his words were understood. 'The LORD said to Moses, "I am going to come to you in a dense cloud in order that the people may hear when I speak with you and so trust you ever after"' (Ex. 19:9). The response is later recorded: 'When all the people witnessed the thunder and lightning, the sound of the trumpet, and the mountain smoking, they were afraid and trembled and stood at a distance, and said to Moses, "You speak to us, and we will listen; but do not let God speak to us, or we will die"' (Ex. 20:18–19).

Other examples include the Lord calling Samuel (1 Sa. 3), and the baptism and transfiguration of Jesus: 'a voice from heaven said . . .', 'from the cloud a voice said . . .' (Mt. 3:17; 17:5). There is an interesting example in John 12 where the voice from heaven replies to Jesus' prayer, 'Father, glorify your name', with the answer, 'I have glorified it, and I will glorify it again', while the crowd hear thunder, and others say an angel has spoken (Jn. 12:28–29). My point is that sometimes when God speaks there is audible sound, and his words are heard. Indeed, I assume that the Old Testament phrase, 'The word of the LORD came to X' (e.g. Je. 1:1–19), often meant that the prophet did hear the audible words of God.

But this is not always the case. In Isaiah 28 we read:

Do those who plough for sowing plough continually?
  Do they continually open and harrow their ground?
When they have levelled its surface,
  do they not scatter dill, sow cummin,
and plant wheat in rows
  and barley in its proper place,
  and spelt as the border?
For they are well instructed;
  their God teaches them.

(Is. 28:23–26)

Here I take it that the instruction and teaching of God did not come by means of audible words, but by observation of farming traditions.

Where there is no audible sound, God communicates directly from his mind to that of the recipient. To describe God as speaking without a physical mouth is no more extraordinary than describing God as delivering or fighting without a physical hand (see *e.g.* 1 Ki. 8:15, 24: 'with his hand', 'with your mouth and with your hand').

Because the language of God's speaking is so foundational to biblical faith, it is then used metaphorically of a wider range of revelation. 'Long ago God spoke to our ancestors in many and various ways by the prophets, but in these last days he has spoken to us by a Son, whom he appointed heir of all things, through whom he also created the worlds' (Heb. 1:1–2). God's speaking through the prophets in 'various ways' included words, signs and visions. And God's speaking through his Son includes his suffering and death, as well as his words.

Should we say that all language about God is metaphorical or analogical? Is Brunner right when he says, 'For when God "speaks", if it really is HE who speaks, something is said which is evidently quite different from that which men usually call "speaking"'?[10] Perhaps it depends on one's understanding of 'quite different'. As Hugo Meynell points out: 'If, for instance, to say that God exists . . . means something totally different from saying that a man exists . . . one might just as well say God does not exist.'[11] May we go so far as to say, with Hendrikus Berkhof, that 'when certain concepts are ascribed to God, they are thus not used figuratively, but in their first and most original sense'?[12] Perhaps this is most obviously true when we talk of God speaking. For God the Trinity is the originator of communication, and men and women made in his image imitate his communication.

Since the idea of God speaking is so fundamental to the Bible, why are we so reluctant to accept it? It is certainly true, as Peter Jensen writes, that 'we would prefer a dumb dark thing, a non-relational far-away god, to be approached on our own terms and worshipped as we see fit'.[13] People prefer a God who does not speak because he makes less clear demands, asks no questions, makes no promises, and threatens no punishments. One reason people prefer the company of dumb animals to that of humans is that dumb animals make fewer demands, ask no questions and make no promises. Nowadays this rejection of the meaning and purpose of God goes even deeper. The postmodern move against meaning in words, and against words themselves, is part of an attempt to create not only a world without God but a universe without meaning.

Rejecting or accepting God's words

The rejection of the words of God is nothing new. Because God is one who speaks, rejection of God will necessarily involve rejection of the words of God. The first temptation to sin begins with the words, 'Did God say . . .?' (Gn. 3:1).

After the law is given on Mount Sinai, and the people sin, the stone tablets with God's words on them are broken as a sign that the newly made covenant has been broken; the remaking of the covenant is later marked by the writing of the words on two new stone tablets (Ex. 32:19; 34:1–27). Moses promises blessings to those who 'obey the LORD your God, by diligently observing all his commandments that I am commanding you today', and curses on those who 'will not obey the LORD your God by diligently observing all his commandments and decrees' (Dt. 28:1, 15).

Later, Joshua is warned: 'This book of the law shall not depart from your mouth; you shall meditate on it day and night, so that you may be careful to act in accordance with all that is written in it' (Jos. 1:8). After King Saul sins, Samuel prophesies:

> Has the LORD as great delight in burnt-offerings and sacrifices,
>   as in obedience to the voice of the LORD?
> Surely, to obey is better than sacrifice,
>   and to heed than the fat of rams.
> For rebellion is no less a sin than divination,
>   and stubbornness is like iniquity and idolatry.
> Because you have rejected the word of the LORD,
>   he has also rejected you from being king.
>
> (1 Sa. 15:22–23)

Jesus says that anyone who hears his words and does not do them is like a man building his house on the sand, whose end is destruction (Mt. 7:24–27), and that if anyone is ashamed of him *and his words* now, the Son of Man will be ashamed of him when he comes in his Father's glory (Mk. 8:38). And Hebrews warns: 'See that you do not refuse the one who is speaking. For if they refused the one who warned them on earth, how much less will we escape if we reject the one who warns from heaven!' (Heb. 12:25).

If the Bible's warning is against rejection of the words of God, its invitation is to accept them. Moses says, 'So now, Israel, give heed to the statutes and ordinances that I am teaching you to observe . . . you must neither add anything to what I command you nor take away anything from it, but keep the commandments of the LORD your God with which I am charging you' (Dt. 4:1–2).

The writer of Proverbs says:

> My child, keep my words
>   and store up my commandments with you;
> keep my commandments and live,
>   keep my teachings as the apple of your eye;
> bind them on your fingers,
>   write them on the tablet of your heart.
>
> (Pr. 7:1–3)

God says through Isaiah: 'This is the one to whom I will look, to the humble and contrite in spirit, who trembles at my word' (Is. 66:2). Jesus says, 'Come to me, all you that are weary and are carrying heavy burdens, and I will give you rest. Take my yoke upon you, and learn from me; for I am gentle and humble in heart, and you will find rest for your souls' (Mt. 11:28–29). Paul asserts that 'faith comes from what is heard, and what is heard comes through the word of Christ' (Rom. 10:17).

My argument so far has been that God has spoken, and that this belief is fundamental to biblical faith. Modern theology has tended to remove the idea of speech from the forms of divine revelation, but I hope I have demonstrated that this is a false move, and that God's words are inseparable from his self-revelation. I have tried to show that the way people respond to God's words is the measure of their response to God. I have spent so much space asserting and defining the idea that God has spoken because without this firm foundation we cannot build a theology of preaching. Without God's words there can be no ministry of the Word. If God is dumb, we may speak, but we cannot speak God's words, for there are none to speak. The first great theological foundation for preaching, then, is that *God has spoken*.

Notes

1. Alan Carefull, *The Priest as Preacher* (Birmingham: Additional Curates Society, n. d.), p. 2.

2. William Herrmann, quoted in John Baillie, *The Idea of Revelation in Recent Thought* (New York: Columbia University Press, 1956), p. 34.

3. William Temple, *Nature, Man and God* (London: Macmillan, 1934), p. 322.

4. See, *e.g.*, John I. Durham, *Exodus*, Word Biblical Commentary (Waco: Word Books, 1987).

5. Avery Dulles, *Models of Revelation* (New York: Image Books, 1985).

6. John Hospers, *An Introduction to Philosophical Analysis* (London: Routledge and Kegan Paul, 2nd edn 1973), pp. 78–79.

7. Paul Helm, *The Divine Revelation* (London: Marshall, Morgan and Scott, 1982), p. 27.

8. Bruce Vawter, *Biblical Inspiration* (London: Hutchinson, 1972).

9. H. D. McDonald, *Ideas of Revelation* (London: Macmillan, 1959); *idem*, *Theories of Revelation* (London: Allen and Unwin, 1962).

10. Emil Brunner, *The Christian Doctrine of God* (Eng. trans. London: Lutterworth, 1949), p. 15.

11. Hugo Meynell, *God and the World* (London: SPCK, 1971), p. 20.

12. Hendrikus Berkhof, *The Christian Faith* (Eng. trans. Grand Rapids: Eerdmans, 1979), p. 69.

13. Peter Jensen, *At the Heart of the Universe* (1991; Leicester: IVP, 1994), p. 83.

2

It is written

The second great foundation for preaching is that *It is written*. This is the belief that in his revelation in history God also preserved his words for future generations. It is on this basis that our teaching and preaching are based on the Bible. On many occasions when God spoke, his intention was not only that his words would constitute revelation to the original audience, but that they would also serve as revelation for future generations.

This of course does not necessarily imply that *all* the prophetic words of Moses or apostolic words of Paul were intended to be preserved. For example the Laodicean letter (Col. 4:16) may have been a letter from Paul that we do not have in our Bibles. These words were revelation, but not subject to preservation. What we have in Scripture is the revealed and preserved words of God.

Other language which is used to describe the activity of God is that of 'inscripturation'[1] and 'fixation'.[2] It is the simple idea that when God spoke he had two audiences in mind, the generation that was present, and future generations (*cf.* Rom. 15:4; 2 Tim. 3:15–16). The fundamental idea is that of preservation: 'inscripturation' describes the method that was either immediately or eventually employed to preserve the words for future generations, and 'fixation' describes the belief that God's revelation is fixed or settled at a particular time for the future.

The Old Testament: words for the future

This forward-looking purpose of revelation is clearly evident in the major themes of the Old Testament. This is so, for example, in the promises made by God to Abraham. While they had meaning and function at the time, they also evidently point forward to generations to come. 'Now the LORD had said to Abram, "Go from your country and your kindred and your father's house to the land I will show you. I will make of you a great nation, and I will bless you, and make your name great, so that you will be a blessing. I will bless those who bless you, and the one who curses you I will curse; and in you all the families of the earth shall be blessed"' (Gn. 12:1–3; *cf.* 15–18).

The first audience of course was Abraham, who obeyed the LORD, and set out from Haran. But the promise did not reach its fulfilment with Abraham. He himself was not a great nation, and the blessing to the nations did not then come through him. 'By faith he stayed for a time in the land he had been promised, as in a foreign land, living in tents, as did Isaac and Jacob, who were heirs with him of the same promise' (Heb. 11:9). If the words of the promise gave meaning and shape to Abraham's obedience, they are of even greater significance for all generations to come: Abraham's physical descendants all through the Old Testament, the Lord Jesus Christ, and the Gentiles who believe in Christ and so become Abraham's children (Gal. 3:6–18). It is a promise not just to Abraham, but for all generations to come. Indeed it could be said that its primary intention was for future generations, and that it is understood most clearly by those who believe in Jesus. It is not only the revelation to Abraham, but the preservation of that revelation for future generations, which is fundamental to the Scriptures and to Christian faith. If we did not know of this promise, our understanding of God's revelation would be immeasurably impoverished.

We do not know when the promise to Abraham was written down, and presumably it was initially preserved in oral form. But its preservation is part of God's plan for the form of his revelation to future generations. If this is true in the covenant of promise with Abraham, it is more clearly evident in the covenant instituted at Mount Sinai. As Edmund Clowney comments:

> The inscripturation of the word of God occurs at Sinai with the establishment of God's covenant with his people. While God's calling of the fathers had a covenant form, the redemption of the assembly of God's people, the congregation of Israel, calls for a formal covenant ratification with a precise and objective covenant instrument in writing.[3]

Moses was the first writing prophet and, on Sinai and beyond, his writing ministry was crucial not only to the institution of the covenant, but also to his ongoing ministry of the Word to the people of Israel until the end of his life.

Words are crucial to the covenant. 'The LORD said to Moses: "Write these words: in accordance with these words I have made a covenant with you and with Israel"' (Ex. 34:27). Clowney notes the background of unilateral covenants between a ruler and his people in Moses' era, which would include the 'words' or requirements that the ruler imposed on the people, the provision of a written copy of the covenant in the sanctuary, and instructions about its regular public reading.[4] The recording of words and instructions for future generations is crucial to biblical revelation. In

Exodus 12, for instance, at the occasion of the Passover, the main preoccupation is the generations to come (Ex. 12:14); no new covenant is made with successive generations.

The response to Moses' reading the written words of the covenant was: 'All that the LORD has spoken we will do' (Ex. 24:7). Forty years later he gave the instruction, 'Assemble the people – men, women and children, as well as the aliens residing in your towns – so they may hear and learn to fear the LORD your God and to observe diligently all the words of this law, and so that their children, who have not known it, may hear and learn to fear the LORD your God, as long as you live in the land that you are crossing over the Jordan to possess' (Dt. 31:12–13). This awareness of the fact that God's address to his people on Mount Sinai is also his address to his people in successive generations is evident in the reading of the law at the time of Josiah (2 Ch. 34) and at the time of Ezra (Ne. 8), and is beautifully expressed in New Testament times in the words of Stephen: Moses 'was in the congregation in the wilderness with the angel who spoke to him at Mount Sinai, and with our ancestors; *and he received living oracles to give to us*' (Acts 7:38). The relationship between the LORD and his covenant people is of course more than words, but the words of the covenant are an integral part of that relationship. And because the covenant lasts, the words must be preserved for future generations.

In the later prophets, the writing ministry continues, especially when the message is of obvious importance for a later generation. 'The word that came to Jeremiah from the LORD: "Thus says the LORD, the God of Israel: Write in a book all the words that I have spoken to you"' (Je. 30:1–2).

> Go now, write it before them on a tablet,
> and inscribe it in a book,
> so that it may be for the time to come
> as a witness for ever.
> (Is. 30:8; *cf.* Hab. 2:2–3; Dn. 9:1–2)

There is, then, evidence of the writing ministry, though it is likely that the majority of the prophets' ministry was spoken to their contemporary audiences, and then written down by the prophets (Is. 8:16) for preservation for future generations. On some occasions the meaning of the prophecy is hidden from present generations: 'The vision of all this has become for you like the words of a sealed document. If it is given to those who can read, with the command, "Read this", they say, "We cannot, for it is sealed"' (Is. 29:11). In most cases, however, the revelation is both for the prophets' contemporaries and also for future generations. Wayne Grudem quotes Lindblom: 'Since the prophets regarded their utterances as Yahweh's words, they thought they were significant for all times.'[5] The wisdom tradition likewise assumes that what has been learnt in previous generations will be of continuing relevance:

> Hear, my child, your father's instruction,
> and do not reject your mother's teaching.
>
> (Pr. 1:8)

The original revelation, then, had its own significance in its day, but it has an even greater significance as it is passed from generation to generation, preserved by God as his revelation for his people. J. I. Packer refers to this as 'cumulative,'[6] and points out that this cumulative revelation becomes self-interpreting. The notion of 'cumulative revelation' is helpful, as long as we recognize that God is the preserver of the revelation, and the one who decides which parts of his revelation will be preserved for future generations, and which parts are of value only to the generation to which they were originally given.

Calvin describes the process of preservation in these terms:

> But whether God became known to the patriarchs through oracles and visions or by the work and ministry of men, he put into their minds what they should then hand down to their posterity. At any rate, there is no doubt that firm certainty of doctrine was engraved in their hearts, so that they were convinced and understood that what they had learned proceeded from God. For by his Word, God rendered faith unambiguous forever, a faith that should be superior to all opinion. Finally, in order that truth might abide forever in the world with a continuing succession of teaching and survive through all ages, the same oracles he had given to the patriarchs it was his pleasure to have recorded, as it were, on public tablets.[7]

This idea of cumulative and public preservation is integral to the notion of historical revelation. If God's acts in history are of saving significance not only for the generations who are involved in them, but also for future generations, then God's explanation of the meaning of the acts will also be of significance for future generations. This means that later ministries of the Word in the Old Testament, as in the prophets, continually call people back to the covenant made on Sinai. These later ministries may also involve reading and applying the historical written documents, as in Ezra's public reading of the law.

The view that the Old Testament is composed of documents preserved by God and forming a cumulative unity is plainly seen in the New Testament. Jesus uses expressions such as 'the law' or 'the prophets' (Mt.

5:17), 'the commandment' or 'the word of God' (Mk. 7:9, 13), or 'the law of Moses, the prophets, and the psalms' (Lk. 24:44). Paul describes the privileges of the Jews in these terms: they 'were entrusted with the oracles of God' (Rom. 3:2); 'to them belong . . . the covenants, the giving of the law . . . and the promises' (Rom. 9:4).

The way the New Testament uses the expressions 'the scripture', 'the scriptures' or 'it is written' makes the point even more clearly. The usage illustrates both the unity of the cumulative revelation, and also the importance of its preservation by inscripturation. Thus Jesus condemns the Sadducees: 'You know neither the scriptures nor the power of God' (Mt. 22:29). He asks the disciples, 'Have you not read this scripture . . .?' (Mk. 12:10). He is concerned to act to fulfil the Scripture: 'How then would the scriptures be fulfilled, which say it must happen in this way?' (Mt. 26:54); 'All this has taken place, so that the scriptures of the prophets may be fulfilled' (Mt. 26:56). In his preaching at Nazareth he declares, 'Today this scripture has been fulfilled in your hearing' (Lk. 4:21). And two disciples describe his ministry by saying that 'he was opening the scriptures to us' (Lk. 24:32). James refers to 'the royal law according to the scripture' (Jas. 2:8), and Paul often refers to 'the scripture', or 'the scriptures' in the course of his letters (Rom. 1:2; 4:3; 9:17; 1 Cor. 15:3; Gal. 3:8, 22). Luke in Acts describes Christian ministry as based on the explanation of the Scriptures: 'Paul . . . argued with them from the scriptures' (Acts 17:2); Apollos was 'well-versed in the scriptures' (Acts 18:24); the Bereans 'examined the scriptures every day' (Acts 17:11).

The New Testament not only assumes the inscripturation of the cumulative revelation, it also believes that because the Old Testament Scriptures point forward to Christ, it is those who believe in the Lord Jesus who are now addressed by God through those same Scriptures. For example: 'These things happened to them to serve as an example, and they were written down to instruct us, on whom the ends of the ages have come' (1 Cor. 10:11). 'For whatever was written in former days was written for our instruction, so that by steadfastness and by the encouragement of the scriptures we might have hope' (Rom. 15:4). In Romans 14:11–12 Paul quotes God's words in Isaiah for his own hearers:

> For it is written,
> > 'As I live, says the Lord, every knee shall bow to me,
> > and every tongue shall give praise to God.'
> So then, each of us will be accountable to God.

Hebrews quotes Proverbs:

> You have forgotten the exhortation that addresses you as children –

'My child, do not regard lightly the discipline of the Lord,
   or lose heart when you are punished by him;
for the Lord disciplines those whom he loves,
   and chastises every child whom he accepts.'

(Heb. 12:5–6)

Jesus uses the words of Isaiah as addressed to Jesus' own contemporaries:

Isaiah prophesied rightly about you hypocrites, as it is written,
   'This people honours me with their lips,
      but their hearts are far from me.'

(Mk. 7:6)

Because New Testament believers are addressed by the cumulative, inscripturated revelation of God in the Old Testament, the New Testament also uses expressions which make it clear that God addresses them and their contemporaries through the words of Scripture. Jesus says,

It is written,
   'One does not live by bread alone,
      but by every word that comes from the mouth of God.'

(Mt. 4:4; cf. Dt. 8:3)

Paul states that Isaiah's words are what 'the Lord has commanded us' (Acts 13:47). Hebrews urges:

Therefore, as the Holy Spirit says,
   'Today, if you hear his voice,
      do not harden your hearts as in the rebellion . . .'

(Heb. 3:7–8)

Paul writes of the law as God speaking to us (1 Cor. 9:9–10). B. B. Warfield can thus point to the interchangeable New Testament expressions 'it says', 'scripture says' and 'God says', and refer to the 'absolute identification by the [New Testament] writers of the Scriptures in their hands [the Old Testament] with the living voice of God'.[8]

New Testament writings

For the writers of the New Testament the Old Testament remains 'the word of God', but they also use this phrase of the message of the gospel. The proconsul Sergius Paulus 'wanted to hear the word of God' (Acts 13:7), Paul claims that 'we refuse to falsify God's word' (2 Cor. 4:2), and church leaders are those 'who spoke the word of God to you' (Heb. 13:7). In Revelation, John is on Patmos 'because of the word of God' (1:9), and martyrs have been 'slaughtered for the word of God' (6:9).

As the Old Testament is the product of the inscripturation of the revelation, and as that revelation continues through the preservation of the inscripturated documents, so the New Testament is the product of the inscripturation of revelation in and about Jesus Christ.

> Since many have undertaken to set down an orderly account of the events that have been fulfilled among us, just as they were handed on to us by those who from the beginning were eyewitnesses and servants of the word, I too decided, after investigating everything carefully from the very first, to write an orderly account for you, most excellent Theophilus, so that you may know the truth of the things about which you have been instructed. (Lk. 1:1–4)

> Jesus did many other signs in the presence of his disciples, which are not written in this book. But these are written so that you may come to believe that Jesus is the Messiah, the Son of God, and that through believing you may have life in his name. (Jn. 20:30–31)

> When this letter has been read among you, have it read also in the church of the Laodiceans and that you read also the letter from Laodicea. (Col. 4:16)

> I appeal to you, brothers and sisters, bear with my word of exhortation, for I have written to you briefly. (Heb. 13:22)

John is instructed, 'Now write what you have seen, what is, and what is to take place after this' (Rev. 1:19). And what is written should be read aloud and heard. 'Blessed is the one who reads aloud the words of the prophecy, and blessed are those who hear and who keep what is written in it; for the time is near' (Rev. 1:3). The New Testament writers knew that the Old Testament was in fact the gospel, the Word of God, now more fully revealed in Jesus Christ.

In view of the importance of inscripturation for the preservation of God's words, we may regard as eccentric Luther's comment: 'That it was necessary to write books is in itself a great breach and decline from the Spirit; it was caused by necessity and not by the proper nature of the New Testament.'[9] On the contrary, we can point out that the New Testament writers created two new literary genres, the gospel and the epistle, in their work of serving not only their own contemporaries but also future generations. For Scripture is 'a living instrument serving God for the proclamation of the message of salvation'.[10] In J. I. Packer's famous phrase, Scripture is 'God preaching'.[11]

The words of Henry Bullinger, the sixteenth-century Swiss Reformer, summarize the message of this chapter:

> The word of God is the speech of God, that is to say, the revealing of his good will to mankind, which from the beginning, one while by his own mouth, and another while by the speech of angels, he did open to those first, ancient, and most holy fathers; who again by tradition did faithfully deliver it to their posterity. Here are to be remembered those great lights of the world, Adam, Seth, Methusalem, Noe, Sem, Abraham, Isaac, Jacob, Amram, and his son Moses, who, at God's commandment, did in writing comprehend the history and traditions of the holy fathers, whereunto he joined the written law, and exposition of the law, together with a large and lightsome history of his own lifetime. After Moses, God gave to his church most excellent men, prophets and priests; who also, by word of mouth and writings, did deliver to their posterity that which they had learned of the Lord. After them came the only-begotten Son of God himself down from heaven into the world, and fulfilled all, whatsoever was found to be written of himself in the law and the prophets. The same also taught a most absolute mean how to live well and holily: he made the apostles his witnesses; which did afterwards first of all with a lively expressed voice preach all things which the Lord had taught them; and then, to the intent that they should not be corrupted, or clean taken out of man's remembrance, they did commit it to writing: so that now we have from the fathers, the prophets, and apostles, the word of God as it was preached and written.[12]

Notes

1. See, *e.g.*, Edmund P. Clowney, *Preaching and Biblical Theology* (New Jersey: Presbyterian and Reformed, n. d.), p. 15; Herman Bavinck, *Our Reasonable Faith* (Grand Rapids: Baker, 1977), p. 104; G. C. Berkouwer, *Holy Scripture* (Grand Rapids: Eerdmans, 1975), pp. 195ff.; D. Broughton Knox, *The Everlasting God* (Welwyn: Evangelical Press, 1982), pp. 18ff.

2. See, *e.g.*, Berkhof, *The Christian Faith*, pp. 77ff.

3. Clowney, *Preaching and Biblical Theology*, p. 39.

4. *Ibid.*, pp. 39–40.

5. Wayne A. Grudem, 'Scripture's Self-Attestation', in D. A. Carson and John D. Woodbridge (eds.), *Scripture and Truth* (Leicester: IVP, 1983), p. 27.

6. J. I. Packer, *God has Spoken* (Grand Rapids: Baker, 1979), pp. 86–87.

7. John Calvin, *Institutes of the Christian Religion* I.vi.2, Library of Christian Classics, vol. 20 (Eng. trans. Philadelphia: Westminster, 1973), p. 71.

8. *The Works of B. B. Warfield*, 1: *Revelation and Inspiration* (Grand Rapids: Baker, 1981), p. 283.

9. Quoted in Berkouwer, *Holy Scripture*, p. 333.

10. *Ibid.*

11. Packer, *God has Spoken*, p. 97.

12. Henry Bullinger, 'The First Decade. Sermon One: Of the Word of God', in *The Decades of Henry Bullinger*, ed. Thomas Harding (Cambridge: Cambridge University Press, 1849), pp. 55–56.

3

Preach the Word

As we have seen, the two great foundations of the ministry of the Word can be summarized in the phrases *God has spoken* and *It is written*. Our third foundation is found in the phrase *Preach the Word*. That is to say, preaching depends not only on having a God-given source, the Bible, but also a God-given commission to preach, teach and explain it to people and to encourage and urge them to respond. The origin of the ministry of the Word is that God has given his words to his servants to pass on to others. This is so familiar that we may fail to give it its due weight. But it is of great significance in the Bible record.

Ministry of the Word is not a great feature of the patriarchal period, though Enoch is referred to as prophesying (Jude 14), and Noah is described as a herald of righteousness (2 Pet. 2:5). Abraham's teaching ministry is described in these words: 'For I have chosen him, that he may charge his children and his household after him to keep the way of the LORD by doing righteousness and justice, so that the LORD may bring about for Abraham what he has promised him' (Gn. 18:19). He is also referred to as a prophet (Gn. 20:7). Another example is Jacob blessing his sons (Gn. 49), and this reminds us that blessings and curses were an early form of verbal ministry. Because they reflected the power of God's words, they were powerful in producing the effect they described, and also irreversible (Gn. 27).

Moses the great minister of the Word

Moses is the great example of God's giving his words to his servant to pass on to others. And it is in Moses' call to this ministry that the relationship between God and his words and his servant is made clear, for we read:

> Moses said to the LORD, 'O my Lord, I have never been eloquent, neither in the past nor even now that you have spoken to your servant; but I am slow of speech and slow of tongue.' Then the LORD said to him, 'Who gives speech to mortals? . . .

Is it not I, the LORD? Now go, and I will be with your mouth and teach you what you are to speak.' But he said, 'O my Lord, please send someone else.' Then the anger of the LORD was kindled against Moses and he said, 'What of your brother, Aaron the Levite? I know he can speak fluently . . . You shall speak to him and put the words in his mouth; and I will be with your mouth and with his mouth, and will teach you what you shall do. He indeed shall speak for you to the people; he shall serve as a mouth for you, and you shall serve as God for him.' (Ex. 4:10–16)

Notice that Moses confesses his inability to speak for God, and that God's reply is that he will help him speak and teach him what to say. This will happen when God gives Moses his words, and then Moses passes them on to Aaron to be his mouth, and Aaron will receive Moses' word as God's words. Despite this arrangement with Aaron, the point is clear, that Moses is God's mouthpiece.

Moses' ministry of the Word to the people of Israel may be examined under four headings.

Moses speaks for God. Moses acts as an intermediary between the LORD and the people at Mount Sinai. We discover that the people did not wish God to speak to them, but wanted Moses to be the one who spoke on God's behalf (Ex. 20:18–19). Thus, 'Moses came and told the people all the words of the LORD and all the ordinances; and all the people answered with one voice, "All the words that the LORD has spoken we will do"' (Ex. 24:3). Later, Moses has the tent of meeting placed outside the camp, where the LORD used to speak to him 'face to face, as one speaks to a friend' (Ex. 33:11). Moses' ministry of the Word is to tell the people of Israel all that he has been commanded (Ex. 34:34). The shape of the ministry of the Word in the Bible is already apparent: God gives his words to his servant, who is to pass them on to others.

Moses writes down the words of God. It is important to note how soon writing became a ministry of the Word. After the LORD gave the Ten Words and the terms of the covenant, we read that 'Moses wrote down all the words of the LORD' (Ex. 24:4). Later, after the people broke the covenant, Moses was commanded, 'Write these words; in accordance with these words I have made a covenant with you and with Israel . . . And he wrote on the tablets the words of the covenant, the ten commandments' (Ex. 34:27–28). There were now two copies of the words of the covenant, both written by Moses. One copy (the 'testimony') is placed in the ark in the tabernacle; the presence of the 'testimony' is so important that the ark is known as the ark of the testimony (Ex. 40:20–21, Hebrew). This is God's copy, and the other is the people's copy, not only for this generation but for generations to come. Moses is the first of the writing prophets.

The presence of the 'testimony' in the ark, later to be placed in the holy of holies, is a sign of the great importance of the words of the covenant.

Later, as the people prepare to enter the promised land, Moses instructs them: 'On the day that you cross over the Jordan into the land that the LORD your God is giving you, you shall set up large stones and cover them with plaster . . . You shall write on the stones all the words of this law very clearly' (Dt. 27:2, 8). Later we read:

> Then Moses wrote down this law, and gave it to the priests, the sons of Levi, who carried the ark of the covenant of the LORD, and to all the elders of Israel . . . When Moses had finished writing down in a book the words of this law to the very end, Moses commanded the Levites . . . 'Take this book of the law and put it beside the ark of the covenant of the LORD your God.' (Dt. 31:9, 24–26)

Moses reads the words of God. If Moses' speaking and writing are part of his ministry of the Word, so too is his reading. At the first making of the Sinai covenant, Moses 'took the book of the covenant, and read it in the hearing of the people' (Ex. 24:7). Later, after Moses had written down his song, he recited it 'in the hearing of the whole assembly of Israel' (Dt. 31:30; 32:44).

Moses the preacher. Moses has the distinction of being the first preacher whose ministry is described for us. We have in Deuteronomy three of Moses' sermons. Notice some important features of Moses' preaching. First, they are an *exposition* of the law given on Mount Sinai. 'Beyond the Jordan in the land of Moab, Moses undertook to expound this law' (Dt. 1:5) – so begins the first sermon. The second begins with a rehearsal of the Ten Commandments (Dt. 5:1–21), and the third sermon has as its subject the covenant of the LORD (Dt. 29). Secondly, Moses *applies* his text to his congregation. It is now forty years since the covenant was made and the LORD gave the law at Sinai. The people are now about to enter the promised land, and Moses is about to die. Moses tells the people in detail what it will mean for them to continue to keep the covenant in the land. Thirdly, Moses *exhorts* the people to obedience. 'So now, Israel, give heed to the statutes and ordinances that I am teaching you . . .' (Dt. 4:1). 'The LORD your God you shall fear; him you shall serve, and by his name alone you shall swear' (Dt. 6:13). 'This entire commandment that I command you today you must diligently observe' (Dt. 8:1). 'So now, O Israel, what does the LORD your God require of you? Only to fear the LORD your God, to walk in all his ways, to love him, to serve the LORD your God with all your heart and with all your soul, and to keep the commandments of the LORD and his decrees that I am commanding you today, for your own well-being' (Dt. 10:12–

13). These three elements of exposition, application and exhortation will again feature in our study: it is fascinating to see them illustrated so early in the history of preaching.

We now have the main ingredients of the ministry of the Word – the servant who hears God's words, the writing down and reading out aloud of God's words, and the preaching of God's words by means of exposition, application, and exhortation.

Moses' ministry of the Word is of great importance to our study, and he is the paradigm prophet in the Bible (Dt. 18:14–22). Indeed, it is possible to see Moses' ministry as the fountain of all Old Testament ministry of the Word. For that ministry was carried on by six groups of people: the *prophets*, who spoke the word of God, recalled people to covenant obedience, and were prophets like Moses; the *priests*, whose ministry of the Word consisted in teaching the law of Moses; the *wise men and women*, who, like Moses, gave instruction about the practical details of living as the covenant people of God (Je. 18:18; 2 Ch. 15:3; Mi. 3:11; Acts 7:22); the *writers of history*, who, like Moses, wrote down the stories of how God dealt with his people (Dt. 1 – 4); the *writers of songs*, who had Moses as their predecessor (Dt. 31:19 – 32:47); and *leaders*, like David, the sweet psalmist of Israel (2 Sa. 23:1), and Solomon, man of wisdom (2 Ch. 1; 1 Ki. 4:29–34).

After Moses

The Old Testament is full of evidence that the tradition of the ministry of the Word that was established in Moses was continued in successive generations. For example, it is said of the prophet Elijah in his ministry to the widow at Zarephath that 'the word of the LORD came to him', and that events happened 'according to the word of the LORD that he spoke by Elijah'. The witness of the woman is: 'Now I know that you are a man of God, and that the word of the LORD in your mouth is truth' (1 Ki. 17:2, 8, 16, 24). The call of the prophet Jeremiah is described in these terms: 'The word of the LORD came to me . . . Then the LORD put out his hand and touched my mouth; and the LORD said to me, "Now, I have put my words in your mouth"' (Je. 1:4, 9). In the call of Ezekiel the words of God came in written form: 'I looked, and a hand was stretched out to me, and a written scroll was in it. He spread it before me; it had writing on the front and on the back, and written on it were words of lamentation and mourning and woe. He said to me, "O mortal, eat what is offered to you, eat this scroll, and go, speak to the house of Israel"' (Ezk. 2:9 – 3:1). Indeed, Amos can say, 'Surely the LORD God does nothing, without revealing his secret to his servants the prophets' (Am. 3:7). The book of Proverbs begins with an invitation to receive the ministry of the Word: 'Hear, my child, your father's instruction, and do not reject your mother's teaching; for they are a fair garland for your head and pendants for your neck' (Pr. 1:8–9).

One of the most striking examples of the ministry of the Word in the Old Testament is the story of the reading of the law in Jerusalem after the return from exile in Babylon. Ezra, who reads the law to all the people, is described as 'the priest . . . the scribe, a scholar of the text of the commandments of the LORD and his statutes for Israel' (Ezr. 7:11). 'Ezra had set his heart to study the law of the LORD, and to do it, and to teach the statutes and ordinances in Israel' (Ezr. 7:10). 'He brought out the book of the law of Moses, stood on a wooden platform, and read it aloud from morning to midday; and all the people listened attentively to it' (Ne. 8:1–4). The Levites (more ministers of the Word) 'helped the people to understand the law, while the people remained in their places. So they read from the book, from the law of God, with interpretation. They gave the sense, so that the people understood the reading' (Ne. 8:7–8). On the next day 'the heads of ancestral houses of all the people, with the priests and the Levites, came together to the scribe Ezra in order to study the words of the law' (Ne. 8:13). And the ministry continued: 'Day by day, from the first day to the last day, [Ezra] read from the book of the law of God' (Ne. 8:18).

Notice the following elements. The priest Ezra, learned in the law, has the ministry of the Word: the ministry is that of the public reading of the law; the law is read to the assembly (it is a ministry to the congregation as a body); the ministry of the Levites is that of translating and interpreting the law (the public reading is followed by a leadership Bible study); and we have the first pulpit in the Bible, capable of supporting thirteen people!

It is worth emphasizing the common elements that we are discovering in the Old Testament ministry of the Word. These include the acceptance of the written or spoken Word as coming from God, the role of 'Scripture', the place of public reading and explanation, encouragement to the right response, and the effect of the ministry on the people. We should not imagine, however, that all ministry of the Word was done by public figures. For at the institution of the ministry of the Word through Moses we have another key element, that of the domestic ministry of the Word. When the Passover was instituted Moses said to the people: 'And when your children ask you, "What do you mean by this observance?" you shall say, "It is the passover sacrifice to the LORD, for he passed over the houses of the Israelites in Egypt, when he struck down the Egyptians but spared our houses"' (Ex. 12:26–27). A more general instruction about the people's responsibility for the domestic ministry of the Word is found in Deuteronomy: 'But take care and watch yourselves closely, so as neither to forget the things that your eyes have seen nor to let them slip from your mind all the days of your life; make them known to your children and your children's children' (Dt. 4:9). One of the purposes of the public reading and teaching of the law, then, is to produce people able to pass it on to the next generation: a domestic or lay ministry of the Word.

A future ministry

We should not finish our brief study of the ministry of the Word in the Old Testament without noting the expectation that the work of God in the future will be accompanied and in part accomplished by ministers of the Word. This is most clearly seen in the latter part of Isaiah, that part of the Old Testament most enthusiastically used by the New Testament.

The return from exile, the new exodus, will again be by means of a divine way through the wilderness. As William Dumbrell points out, 'this will happen as a result of the proclamation of the divine Word',[1] as we see in Isaiah 40:3 (see Mk. 1:3; Lk. 3:6; Jn. 1:23):

> A voice cries out:
> 'In the wilderness prepare the way of the LORD
>   make straight in the desert a highway for our God.'

Despite human frailty and weakness, 'the word of our God will stand for ever' (Is. 40:8; *cf.* 1 Pet. 1:25). The announcement is by means of a human messenger of the Word:

> Get you up to a high mountain,
>   O Zion, herald of good tidings;
> lift up your voice with strength,
>   O Jerusalem, herald of good tidings,
>   lift it up, do not fear;
> say to the cities of Judah,
>   'Here is your God!'

(Is. 40:9)

The servant of the LORD has a work to do which includes the ministry of the Word:

> The spirit of the LORD God is upon me,
>   because the LORD has anointed me;
> he has sent me to bring good news to the oppressed,
>   to bind up the broken-hearted,
> to proclaim liberty to the captives,
>   and release to the prisoners;
> to proclaim the year of the LORD's favour,
>   and the day of vengeance of our God.

(Is. 61:1–2)

This ministry is not only to Israel, but also to the Gentiles:

> It is too light a thing that you should be my servant
> > to raise up the tribes of Jacob
> > and to restore the survivors of Israel;
> I will give you as a light to the nations,
> > that my salvation may reach to the ends of the earth.
>
> (Is. 49:6)

It is fascinating to note how the New Testament sees these two verses. The first is applied to the Lord Jesus and his ministry (Lk. 4:18–19), and the second is used by Paul and his friends as a defence of their own ministry to the Gentiles (Acts 13:47). The Servant's ministry of the Word is the daily gift of God:

> The LORD God has given me
> > the tongue of a teacher,
> that I may know how to sustain
> > the weary with a word.
> Morning by morning he wakens –
> > wakens my ear
> > to listen as those who are taught.
>
> (Is. 50:4)

Isaiah states the dilemma of all preachers of the Word: 'Who has believed what we have heard? And to whom has the arm of the LORD been revealed?' (Is. 53:1; *cf.* Rom. 10:16). But he affirms his confidence in the power of God in his Word:

> For as the rain and snow come down from heaven,
> > and do not return there until they have watered the earth,
> making it bring forth and sprout,
> > giving seed to the sower and bread to the eater,
> so shall my word be that goes out from my mouth;
> > it shall not return to me empty,
> but it shall accomplish that which I purpose,
> > and succeed in the thing for which I sent it.
>
> (Is. 55:10–11)

The new covenant will be a time of knowledge of the words of God. 'As for me, this is my covenant with them, says the LORD: my spirit that is upon you, and my words that I have put in your mouth, shall not depart out of your mouth, or out of the mouths of your children, or out of the mouths of your children's children, says the LORD, from now on and for ever' (Is. 59:21; partly quoted in Rom. 11:27). For God's delight is in those who receive and live by his words. 'This is the one to whom I will look, to the humble and contrite in spirit, who trembles at my word' (Is. 66:2b). And God's people will recognize the beauty of God's messengers.

> How beautiful upon the mountains
> > are the feet of the messenger who announces peace,
> who brings good news,
> > who announces salvation,
> > who says to Zion, 'Your God reigns.'
> > > > (Is. 52:7; *cf.* Rom. 10:15)

The message of God's justice, reign and glory will go to the ends of the earth. 'From them I will send survivors to the nations, to Tarshish, Put, and Lud – which draw the bow – to Tubal and Javan, to the coastlands far away that have not heard of my fame or seen my glory; and they shall declare my glory among the nations' (Is. 66:19). The coming of the gospel to the nations through the work and words of Christ, and through the words of his messengers, is here foretold through the ministry of Isaiah. Part of Isaiah's ministry of the Word is to point forward to the great ministry of the Word that will be the preaching of the gospel to the nations.

John the Baptist

The New Testament opens with the ministry of the Word of John the Baptist:

> The beginning of the good news of Jesus Christ, the Son of God. As it is written in the prophet Isaiah,
> > 'See, I am sending my messenger ahead of you,
> > > who will prepare your way:
> > the voice of one crying out in the wilderness:
> > > "Prepare the way of the Lord,
> > > make his paths straight."'
> John the baptizer appeared in the wilderness, proclaiming a baptism of repentance for the forgiveness of sins. (Mk. 1:1–4)

John's ministry of the Word is defined by Scripture, and he also uses that same Scripture as part of his message (Is. 40:3; Jn. 1:23). His message includes application and exhortation:

> John said to the crowds that came out to be baptized by him, 'You brood of vipers! Who warned you to flee from the wrath to come? Bear fruits worthy of repentance. Do not begin to say to

yourselves, "We have Abraham as our ancestor"; for I tell you, God is able from these stones to raise up children to Abraham. Even now the axe is lying at the root of the trees; every tree therefore that does not bear good fruit is cut down and thrown into the fire.' (Lk. 3:7–9)

John's message also focuses on the Lord Jesus. 'The next day [John] saw Jesus coming towards him and declared, 'Here is the Lamb of God, who takes away the sin of the world!' (Jn. 1:29). John was 'a burning and shining lamp', but when Jesus' ministry begins, John says, 'He must increase, but I must decrease' (Jn. 5:35; 3:30).

Jesus

In our study of Jesus' ministry of the Word, we shall look at the first few chapters of Mark's gospel, noting Mark's emphasis on Jesus' teaching and preaching.

Mark opens his document, as we have seen, with the words: 'The beginning of the good news of Jesus Christ, the Son of God' (Mk. 1:1). The 'good news of Jesus Christ' which Mark wants to convey begins with the ministry of John the Baptist, but it is Jesus Christ whose ministry and death and resurrection form the content of the gospel. Jesus' ministry of the Word is a crucial part of this ministry, not merely an accidental commentary on it. The kingdom comes, in part, by means of Jesus' preaching. 'After John was arrested, Jesus came to Galilee, proclaiming the good news of God, and saying, "The time is fulfilled, and the kingdom of God has come near; repent, and believe in the good news"' (Mk. 1:14–15). In these words Jesus summarizes the Old Testament as his 'text' (the 'time', the 'kingdom'), and applies it to his hearers, exhorting them to respond ('repent, and believe'). With this formative portrait of Jesus the preacher, Mark begins his account of Jesus' ministry.

Mark uses many different phrases in chapters 1 – 3 to describe Jesus' ministry of the Word. 'Follow me,' Jesus said; 'he called them'; 'he entered the synagogue and taught' (Mk. 1:17, 20–21).

Mark shows us that Jesus' life and ministry evoke wonder and amazement, but this amazement begins with response to Jesus' teaching. 'They were astounded at his teaching.' 'They were all amazed and they kept on asking one another, "What is this? A new teaching – with authority! He commands even the unclean spirits, and they obey him"' (Mk. 1:22, 27). At this stage, preaching is Jesus' priority: 'He answered, "Let us go on to the neighbouring towns, so that I may proclaim the message there also; for that is what I came out to do"' (Mk. 1:38).

Mark's summary of Jesus' teaching ministry continues: 'When Jesus returned to Capernaum after some days, it was reported that he was at home. So many gathered around that there was no longer room for them not even in front of the door; and he was speaking the word to them' (Mk. 2:1–2). 'Jesus went out again beside the lake; the whole crowd gathered around him, and he taught them' (Mk. 2:13). In addition to his public ministry, Mark also pictures Jesus as engaged in responsive teaching during dinner, in the cornfields and in the synagogue (Mk. 2:23–27). This too is part of Jesus' ministry of the Word, as he answers questions from opponents, enquirers and his disciples.

With the parable of the seeds in chapter 4, Jesus describes and links his own ministry of the Word, the growth of the kingdom of God, and the ministry of the Word of his disciples. 'A sower went out to sow.' The seed is clearly explained as 'the word'. 'The sower sows the word . . . the ones sown on the good soil . . . hear the word and accept it, and bear fruit . . .' (Mk. 4:1–20). 'Someone . . . [scatters] seed on the ground.' 'The kingdom of God . . . is like a mustard seed' (Mk. 4:26, 31).

Then Mark summarizes Jesus' dual ministry of the Word: to the crowds ('With many such parables he spoke the word to them'); and to the disciples ('he explained everything in private to his disciples') (Mk. 4:33–34). In view of this detailed picture of Jesus' preaching and teaching ministry, it is no wonder that at his transfiguration, the voice from the cloud says, 'This is my Son, the Beloved; *listen to him!*' (Mk. 9:7).

In the other gospels too, Jesus is the minister of the Word. Matthew includes chapters of Jesus' teaching, and describes Jesus' last commission to his disciples as including the task of 'teaching them to obey everything that I have commanded you' (Mt. 28:20). In John, Jesus summarizes his teaching ministry: 'The words that you gave to me I have given to them, and they have received them' (Jn. 17:8). In Acts, Luke describes his gospel as containing 'all that Jesus did and taught . . . giving instructions through the Holy Spirit to the apostles whom he had chosen' (Acts 1:1–2). So it is appropriate for Luke to mark the beginning of Jesus' public ministry in chapter 4 of his gospel with the general statement, 'he began to teach in their synagogues' (Lk. 4:15), followed by the specific description of Jesus' ministry in the synagogue at Nazareth.

Before we look at Luke's account of Jesus' ministry, it might be helpful to remind ourselves of the general pattern of the ministry of the Word in the synagogues in the first century. As far as we can tell, the service included the following elements: the public confession of the Shema (Dt. 6:4–9; 11:13–21); prayers; a reading from the Torah (in Hebrew of course, and a paraphrase in Aramaic); a reading from the Prophets (like the reading from the Torah, according to a lectionary); a prayer; a sermon (if there was someone present who was qualified to teach); and a prayer. With this outline in mind, we can understand the context and content of Jesus' ministry. Note that it was twofold: it included both reading and teaching.

When he came to Nazareth, where he had been brought up, he went to the synagogue on the sabbath day, as was his custom. He stood up to read, and the scroll of the prophet Isaiah was given to him. He unrolled the scroll and found the place where it was written:

'The Spirit of the Lord is on me,
because he has anointed me
to bring good news to the poor.
He has sent me to proclaim release to the captives
and recovery of sight to the blind,
to let the oppressed go free,
to proclaim the year of the Lord's favour.'

And he rolled up the scroll, gave it back to the attendant, and sat down. The eyes of all in the synagogue were fixed on him. Then he began to say to them, 'Today this scripture has been fulfilled in your hearing.' (Lk. 4:16–21)

Jesus' ministry included that of reading the lectionary passage from the Prophets. Note that he chose this reading, and that it was a reading which contained a strong emphasis on the ministry of the Word: 'to bring good news . . . to proclaim'. In his teaching, Jesus applied the message to his hearers: 'Today this Scripture has been fulfilled in your hearing.' Again we note that the ministry of the Word includes both the historic revelation and the contemporary application.

I have been emphasizing Jesus' ministry of the Word. I am not claiming that this ministry was all that Jesus did, or that it was the most important of his actions. His ministry included various miracles, and his death and resurrection were obviously of central importance. But his preaching and teaching were also an integral and essential part of his ministry and revelation. Jesus was a minister of the Word.

We should notice too the variety of forms in which Jesus ministered the Word. In public, formal teaching in synagogues or on the mountain, in private instruction to his disciples, in answer to questions raised by others, and in private conversations, he spoke the Word. By his preaching and teaching he both announced and extended the kingdom, called people to faith, refuted error, rebuked those who taught error, encouraged the weak, trained his disciples, explained the Scripture, rebuked sinners and summoned all to faith and obedience.

The disciples

Not only is Jesus a minister of the Word, but central to his strategy is the calling of others to that ministry. 'He appointed twelve, whom he also named apostles, to be with him, and to be sent out to proclaim the message, and to have authority to cast out demons' (Mk. 3:14–15). Because of Jesus' compassion on the crowds he encourages his disciples to ask the Lord of the harvest to send out labourers into his harvest field (Mt. 9:36–38). As the disciples travel around, their instruction is to preach the message of the kingdom (Mt. 10:7). As Jesus' messengers, their ministry will be effective: 'Whoever welcomes you welcomes me, and whoever welcomes me welcomes the one who sent me' (Mt. 10:40).

The disciples' ministry of preaching the kingdom is ultimately and inextricably linked with their right understanding of both the Old Testament, and Jesus' death and resurrection. On the road to Emmaus: 'He said to them, "Oh, how foolish you are, and how slow of heart to believe all that the prophets have declared! Was it not necessary that the Messiah should suffer these things and then enter into his glory?" Then beginning with Moses and all the prophets, he interpreted to them the things about himself in all the scriptures' (Lk. 24:25–27). And later: '"These are my words that I spoke to you while I was still with you – that everything written about me in the law of Moses, the prophets, and the psalms must be fulfilled." Then he opened their minds to understand the scriptures, and he said to them, "Thus it is written, that the Messiah is to suffer and to rise from the dead on the third day, and that repentance and forgiveness of sins is to be proclaimed in his name to all nations, beginning from Jerusalem. You are witnesses of these things"' (Lk. 24:44–48).

During Jesus' ministry on earth, the disciples received his word: 'Those who love me will keep my word, and my Father will love them, and we will come to them and make our home with them. Whoever does not love me does not keep my words; and the word that you hear is not mine, but is from the Father who sent me' (Jn. 14:23–24). After Jesus' death and resurrection, the Holy Spirit, the Counsellor, would continue this ministry to these disciples: 'I have said these things to you while I am still with you. But the Advocate, the Holy Spirit, whom the Father will send in my name, will teach you everything, and remind you of all that I have said to you' (Jn. 14:25–26).

As we have seen, the final commission to the disciples in Matthew 28 contains a strong emphasis on their ministry of the Word springing out of Jesus' ministry of the Word. They are to make disciples of all nations, and teach them to obey all that Jesus has commanded (Mt. 28:18–20).

The apostles

We have discovered that God's giving his servants his words to pass on to others is a strong feature of revelation both under the old covenant and in the ministry of Jesus. It will come as no surprise, therefore, to find out that the ministry of the Word continues and increases after Pentecost.

We begin by looking at the evidence from Acts. The implication of 1:1, 'In the first book . . . I wrote about all that Jesus did and taught . . .' is that Acts is the story of Jesus' continued ministry from heaven of doing and teaching. The great day of Pentecost, the first day of apostolic ministry, is focused on a sermon. The occasion of the sermon is the wind, fire and tongues given by the Holy Spirit; the preacher is Peter on behalf of the twelve apostles; the audience is the crowd; the content is the interpretation of Old Testament Scripture and the story of Jesus; the application is 'Repent, and be baptized'; the sermon ends with exhortation, warning and pleading; and its result is that about 3,000 welcomed Peter's message and were baptized and added to the number of disciples.

For Luke, this is not only the beginning of apostolic ministry, but also its model, as we discover throughout Acts. 'When they had prayed, the place in which they were gathered together was shaken; and they were all filled with the Holy Spirit and spoke the word of God with boldness' (Acts 4:31). 'They entered the temple at daybreak and went on with their teaching. When the high priest and those with him arrived, they called together the council and the whole body of the elders of Israel, and sent to the prison to have them brought' (Acts 5:21).

The priority of the ministry of the Word for the twelve is clearly demonstrated in Acts 6: 'The twelve called together the whole community of the disciples and said, 'It is not right that we should neglect the word of God in order to wait at tables. Therefore, friends, select from among yourselves seven men of good standing, full of the Spirit and of wisdom, whom we may appoint to this task, while we, for our part, will devote ourselves to prayer and to serving the word'' (Acts 6:2–4). And the result of this strategy is that 'The word of God continued to spread; the number of disciples increased greatly in Jerusalem, and a great many of the priests became obedient to the faith' (Acts 6:7). With the conversion and commission of Saul (Paul), this ministry of the Word continues and increases in scope. For within several days of his conversion 'he began to proclaim Jesus in the synagogues, saying, "He is the Son of God"' (Acts 9:20).

Luke's account continues with many descriptions of Paul's ministry of preaching and teaching. 'Saul became increasingly more powerful and confounded the Jews who lived in Damascus by proving that Jesus was the Messiah' (Acts 9:22). Later, 'He went in and out among them in Jerusalem, speaking boldly in the name of the Lord. He spoke and argued with the Hellenists; but they were attempting to kill him' (Acts 9:28–29).

When Barnabas and Saul are sent out by the church in Antioch we read, 'When they arrived at Salamis, they proclaimed the word of God in the synagogues of the Jews' (Acts 13:5), and later, 'In Iconium . . . Paul and Barnabas went into the Jewish synagogue and spoke in such a way that a great number of both Jews and Greeks became believers' (Acts 14:1). In Acts 13, we read an account of one of Paul's synagogue sermons, including a summary of Old Testament history and the story of Jesus, exegesis of some verses from the Psalms, and application and exhortation to his hearers.

J. A. Motyer[2] claims that Paul's description of his ministry in Acts 15:7 provides an important clue for understanding the task of all preaching. 'God made a choice among you, that I should be the one through whom the Gentiles would hear the message of the good news and become believers.' Motyer draws attention to God's choice, the lips and mouth of the preacher, the response of hearing the word of the gospel, and the response of faith.

Acts ends with this description of Paul: 'He lived [in Rome] two whole years at his own expense and welcomed all who came to him, proclaiming the kingdom of God and teaching about the Lord Jesus Christ with all boldness and without hindrance' (Acts 28:30–31). Paul describes his own ministry in terms of proclamation and teaching: 'Christ did not send me to baptize but to proclaim the gospel, and not with eloquent wisdom, so that the cross of Christ might not be emptied of its power' (1 Cor. 1:17). 'We proclaim Christ crucified, a stumbling-block to Jews and foolishness to Gentiles, but to those who are the called, both Jews and Greeks, Christ the power of God and the wisdom of God' (1 Cor. 1:23–24). 'We do not proclaim ourselves; we proclaim Jesus Christ as Lord, and ourselves as your slaves for Jesus' sake' (2 Cor. 4:5). 'It is him whom we proclaim, warning everyone and teaching everyone in all wisdom, so that we may present everyone mature in Christ. For this I toil and struggle with all the energy that he powerfully inspires within me' (Col. 1:28–29). 'For this I was appointed a herald and an apostle (I am telling the truth, I am not lying), and a teacher of the Gentiles in faith and truth' (1 Tim. 2:7).

In 1 John 1:1–3, too, we find an apostolic ministry of the Word in terms of declaration and testimony:

> We declare to you what was from the beginning, what we have heard, what we have seen with our eyes, what we have looked at and touched with our hands, concerning the word of life – this life was revealed, and we have seen it and testify to it, and declare to you the eternal life that was with the Father and was revealed to us – we declare what we have seen and heard so that you also may have fellowship with us; and truly our fellowship is with the Father and with his Son Jesus Christ.

It is appropriate to mention at this point the evidence from Revelation. The book describes itself as a 'prophecy', and it is prophecy which is written down, to be read aloud, presumably in the seven Christian congregations of Asia Minor: 'Blessed is the one who reads aloud the words of the prophecy, and blessed are those who hear it and who keep what is written in it; for the time is near' (Rev. 1:3). The prophecy written in the book has divine authority: 'I warn everyone who hears the words of the prophecy of this book: if anyone adds to them, God will add to that person the plagues described in this book; if anyone takes away from the words of this book of prophecy, God will take away that person's share in the tree of life and in the holy city, which are described in this book' (Rev. 22:18–19).

The process of revelation outlined in the book follows the sequence God – Jesus Christ – angel – John – reader – hearers. The revelation comes in the form of a vision, so the repeated instruction is: 'Write in a book what you see . . . Now write what you have seen, what is, and what is to take place after this' (Rev. 1:11, 19). This pattern is familiar to us, though it contains its particular emphasis. The revelation comes from God, it is given to the prophet, and it is written down so that it may be read and heard by the people of God.

In the light of the references in Revelation, it is worth reminding ourselves that writing was a key element in the ministry of the Word of the apostles. They were not only preachers but writers, thus carrying on the prophetic and historic ministry begun by Moses, and making their ministry available not only to distant readers of their own day but also to future generations. John's gospel comes to its conclusion with these words:

> Jesus did many other signs in the presence of his disciples, which are not written in this book. But these are written that you may come to believe that Jesus is the Messiah, the Son of God, and that through believing you may have life in his name . . . This is the disciple who is testifying to these things and has written them down, and we know that his testimony is true. But there are also many other things that Jesus did; if every one of them were written down, I suppose that the world itself could not contain the books that would be written. (Jn. 20:30–31; 21:24–25)

The apostles were undoubtedly ministers of the Word. But they had no exclusive claim on that ministry in the post-Pentecost church; in fact their ministry had as one of its aims a proliferation of the ministry of the Word in all the churches.

Other ministers of the Word

The post-Pentecost proliferation of the speaking of God's truth among not only Jewish but also Gentile believers in Jesus Christ is signalled by Peter's use of the words of Joel 2:28–32 in his Pentecost sermon:

> In the last days it will be, God declares,
> that I will pour out my Spirit upon all flesh,
>   and your sons and your daughters shall prophesy,
> and your young men shall see visions,
>   and your old men shall dream dreams.
> Even upon my slaves, both men and women,
>   in those days I will pour out my Spirit;
>   and they shall prophesy.
>
> (Acts 2:17–18)

Here is the promise that God will pour out his Spirit on all people, and that one of the results of this will be that they speak words from God. Every believer, then, has a word ministry, if not a formal ministry of the Word. We discover in Acts that when persecution breaks out against the church in Jerusalem, all except the apostles are scattered through Judea and Samaria, and 'those who were scattered went from place to place, proclaiming the word' (Acts 8:4).

Even those chosen by the apostles to wait at tables (Acts 6:2) have a ministry of the Word. Stephen in his speech to the Sanhedrin gives a great example of an effective sermon, including as it does the purposeful and theological use of the Old Testament, and the direct application to his hearers: 'You stiff-necked people, uncircumcised in heart and ears, you are for ever opposing the Holy Spirit, just as your ancestors used to do. Which of the prophets did your ancestors not persecute? They killed those who foretold the coming of the Righteous One, and now you have become his betrayers and murderers' (Acts 7:51–52). In Acts 8 we read of Philip, another of the seven, who meets the Ethiopian eunuch and explains to him the meaning of Isaiah 53: 'Philip . . . starting with this scripture . . . proclaimed to him the good news about Jesus' (Acts 8:35). Here again in Acts the ministry of the Word includes the explanation of Scripture, the Old Testament, in terms of the gospel of Jesus. Priscilla and Aquila also explain the Way of God to Apollos at their home (Acts 18: 26), and then Apollos continues his ministry. 'He powerfully refuted the Jews in public, showing by the scriptures that the Messiah is Jesus' (Acts 18:28).

Part of Paul's strategy was to build up a team of ministers of the Word, and an obvious member of that team in Acts is Barnabas. Barnabas was a native of Cyprus, and a Levite. (We have already noticed that the teaching responsibility of the Levites is established in the Old Testament; see 2 Ch. 17:7–9; Ne. 8). His name is first Joseph, but he is renamed Barnabas (Acts 4:36–37) which means 'son of encouragement'.

The ministry of Barnabas and Paul is described in this characteristic way in Acts:

> As Paul and Barnabas were going out, the people urged them to speak about these things again the next sabbath. When the meeting of the synagogue broke up, many Jews and devout converts to Judaism followed Paul and Barnabas, who spoke to them and urged them to continue in the grace of God. The next sabbath almost the whole city gathered to hear the word of the Lord. (Acts 13:42–44)

Later, at Iconium,

> Paul and Barnabas went into the Jewish synagogue and spoke in such a way that a great number of Jews and Greeks became believers . . . they remained for a long time, speaking boldly for the Lord, who testified to the word of his grace by granting signs and wonders to be done through them. (Acts 14:1, 3).

Luke also refers to the many who wrote down their accounts of the coming of Christ and the growth of the churches: 'Many have undertaken to set down an orderly account of the events that have been fulfilled among us, just as they were handed on to us by those who from the beginning were eyewitnesses and servants of the word' (Lk. 1:1–2).

Everyone, then, has some kind of ministry of the Word. It is likely that in Ephesians Paul refers to the function of teaching elders in equipping people for these ministries: 'The gifts he gave were that some would be . . . pastors and teachers, to equip the saints for the work of ministry, for building up the body of Christ . . . speaking the truth in love, we must grow up in every way into him who is the head, into Christ . . .' (Eph. 4:11–12, 15). Paul includes others in his apostolic ministry, that is, in the work of the gospel. Prisca and Aquila work with him (Rom. 16:3), as do Urbanus (Rom: 16:9), Timothy (Rom. 16:21), Epaphroditus (Phil. 2:25), Euodia, Syntyche and Clement (Phil. 4:2–4), Aristarchus, Mark, Jesus called Justus, and Epaphras (Col. 4:10–12). In Colossians 3:16 Paul encourages the believers to 'let the word of Christ dwell in you richly; teach and admonish one another in all wisdom; and with gratitude in your hearts sing psalms, hymns and spiritual songs to God'.

Hebrews 10 exhorts us to a similar ministry of words: ': . . not neglecting to meet together, as is the habit of some, but encouraging one another, and all the more as you see the Day approaching' (Heb. 10:25).

Peter teaches his congregation: 'Like good stewards of the manifold grace of God, serve one another with whatever gift each of you has received. Whoever speaks must do so as one speaking the very words of God; whoever serves must do so with the strength that God supplies, so that God may be glorified in all things through Jesus Christ' (1 Pet. 4:10–11).

Christian communities after the apostles will be communities in which the ministry of the Word continues, both through the work of the teaching elders, and through the ministry of all the members of the churches.

The ministry of the Word after the apostles: teaching elders

It is of course of great interest to us to discover what kind of ministry of the Word is appropriate after the apostles. As we have seen, there are varieties of types of ministry at different stages throughout the Bible, ranging from Old Testament prophets and priests to New Testament disciples, prophets and apostles. The question remains: what model is appropriate today? When I refer to ministry of the Word after the apostles, I use the phrase in both a local and also a wider historical sense. In a local sense, it is that kind of ministry of the Word which the apostles left after they had evangelized an area and planted a church. In a wider sense, it is that provision that God made for a continued ministry of the Word after the time of the apostles of Christ, the witnesses of his resurrection. As Wayne Grudem claims, 'the apostles are the New Testament counterpart of the divinely authoritative Old Testament prophets'.[3] Then, when both groups have finished their ministry, their message needs to be taught to succeeding generations.

Hence the appointment of teaching elders. The office of the elders derived from Judaism, where it was a common feature of political and religious life, especially centred on the synagogue as a focus of the local community. In Acts 11:30 we read of 'the elders' of the church in Judea, and in Acts 15:6 of a meeting of the apostles and elders in Jerusalem, which resulted in a letter to Gentile believers from 'the brothers, both the apostles and the elders' (Acts 15:23). Evidently Paul began the custom of appointing elders even in largely established Gentile churches (Acts 14:23), and Paul's address to the Ephesian elders includes these words describing what ministry he expects of them: 'Keep watch over yourselves and over all the flock, of which the Holy Spirit has made you overseers, to shepherd the church of God that he obtained with the blood of his own Son' (Acts 20:28). Elsewhere Paul makes it clear that a congregation without elders is incomplete (Tit. 1:5). Paul's instruction to Timothy is, 'Let the elders who rule well be considered worthy of double honour, especially those who labour in preaching and teaching' (1 Tim. 5:17).

This task is reflected in the gift of 'pastors and teachers' in Ephesians 4:11.

Peter too addresses the leaders of the churches of Asia Minor: 'I exhort the elders among you to tend the flock of God that is in your charge, exercising the oversight' (1 Pet. 5:1–2). There seem to have been leaders described as elders or overseers in many New Testament churches. Their task of feeding or teaching is of crucial importance in the early church. This role of teaching elders is also reflected in Hebrews 13:7: 'Remember your leaders, those who spoke the word of God to you; consider the outcome of their way of life, and imitate their faith.' It is also seen in 2 and 3 John, where 'the elder' is concerned about 'the truth'.

It is important to recognize that those appointed had a twofold, inter-connected role: as elders they had responsibility in and for a congregation, and as teachers their task was clearly though not exhaustively defined. They were not freelance teachers, nor were they elders without teaching responsibility. Others may have taught, and evidently others were elders, but this role was definitely that of teaching elders. We will see in the next chapter what characteristics are essential for these teaching elders.

In this chapter we have been laying the third great foundation of preaching. *God has spoken*, *It is written*, and God has also instructed us to *Preach the Word*. God is the source of our preaching: he provided his words, spoken long ago and written down for us, and he has instructed his servants to preach and teach them to his people.

In Part 2 we shall build a practical theology of preaching on this firm theological foundation. But we now end Part 1 with some implications to stimulate further reflection.

Implications

God speaks. God's self-revelation includes words which are intended to communicate. The ability to communicate in words is an aspect of our creation in God's image. We should value words as a gift of God, especially since we may use words that God has spoken to understand and relate to him, and since we may use words to communicate about God to others.

God's words are effective. Because they are words that God has spoken, they have all the power of God, the speaker, behind them and within them. Our role is not to make God's words powerful through our speaking, but to help people recognize the power and significance of those words.

God's words are part of his self-revelation. God's words are not remote from him: he is present in his words. Our preaching of God's words is not an invitation to consider something remote from God, but an invitation to meet the living God in his words.

God has appointed the ministry of the Word. Human servants are God's main means for making his words known. Preachers are not an intrusion, nor are they unnecessary in an obedient church; they are God's method of bringing his words to Christian and non-Christian alike.

God has preserved his words for us today. God wrote the Bible with us in mind. It is an ancient book, but it is also 'God preaching'. We need to work on how it is relevant, but we may assume that it is relevant, and that it contains God's message for today.

God has human agents in giving his revelation and preserving his words. When we are teaching and preaching the Bible, we shall need to take into account the one divine mind behind it, its one divine author, and thus recognize its unity, authority and power. We also need to respect its varied human authors, and the historical and theological context in which each separate part was written.

God's revelation is both historical and contemporary. Our preaching of the Bible should not be merely historical (without contemporary application) or merely contemporary (with no regard to its historical context and meaning). Rather, we should reflect the two audiences God had in mind: the original hearers of the words, and those for whom the words are preserved, including ourselves. Good preaching will be firmly grounded in both eras, understanding the words in their biblical context, and applying them today as God intended.

Notes

1. William Dumbrell, *The Faith of Israel* (Grand Rapids: Baker, 1988; Leicester: Apollos, 1989), p. 108.

2. J. A. Motyer, Foreword, in Haddon W. Robinson, *Expository Preaching: Principles and Practice* (Leicester: IVP, 1986), p. ii.

3. Wayne Grudem, *The Gift of Prophecy* (Eastbourne: Kingsway, 1988), p. 32.

Part 2

The preacher at work

4

Preaching as a ministry of the Word

In Part 1 we looked at the biblical origin of preaching with the great foundation doctrines found in the Bible: *God has spoken*, *It is written* and *Preach the Word*. Having established the theological foundations for preaching, we now look at different aspects of the preacher's task, both in preparation and in presentation. In this chapter we will be looking at preaching as one of many ministries of the Word, and at what we can learn from the New Testament about preaching. In chapter 5, we shall study some issues that confront the preacher when tackling the Bible; in chapter 6 we try to define the purpose of preaching, and in chapter 7 we identify its demands.

Many ministries of the Word

By 'preaching' we mean something like 'a public formal monologue to the congregation' (to use a sociological definition), or, in Anthony Hoekstra's words, 'the administration of the Word in the assembled congregation of Christ'[1] (a more theological definition). I will use Hoekstra's description as my basis, but it will need some changes to make it more satisfactory. (Almost every book on preaching quotes Phillips Brooks's definition of preaching as 'truth through personality'.[2] But this is general enough to include the stand-up comic or a good actor!) While preaching, according to this definition, is one form of the ministry of the Word, many other forms are reflected in the Bible and in contemporary Christian church life. It is important to grasp this point clearly, or we shall try to make preaching carry a load which it cannot bear; that is, the burden of doing all that the Bible expects of every form of ministry of the Word. Also, we shall unduly limit what we read in the Bible by putting it through the narrow grid of our understanding of what 'preaching' is.

A moment's reflection about the ministry of Jesus will help us to realize that there were many different ways in which Jesus ministered the Word to the people of his generation. He was of course a public teacher, preaching to the crowds and teaching them about the kingdom of God. This public ministry of proclamation is described in these words: 'Jesus came to Galilee, proclaiming the good news of God, and saying, "The time is fulfilled, and the kingdom of God has come near; repent and believe in the good news"' (Mk. 1:14–15). But in addition to this public proclamation there is also Jesus' private teaching or training of his disciples. We read at the beginning of the account of the Sermon on the Mount: 'When Jesus saw the crowds, he went up the mountain; and after he sat down, his disciples came to him. Then he began to speak, and taught them' (Mt. 5:1–2). Jesus' ministry of the Word to his disciples was of course of great importance. We would not normally describe that as 'preaching', but rather the teaching of a small group or the training of disciples. There are also occasions recorded in the gospels in which Jesus engages in a ministry of the Word to an individual. In John 4 Jesus' discussion with the Samaritan woman is certainly a ministry of the Word directed to one person. The point I am making is that ministry of the Word is a general description which covers a variety of ministries, of which the public formal monologue to a crowd or congregation is only one.

Paul's ministry too is that of a public teacher and preacher, but he also engages in other forms of ministry of the Word, especially in his writing of letters.

In the church today the following activities can be described as various ministries of the Word.

Evangelizing unbelievers is a ministry of the Word, whether that takes place on a public occasion or in a conversation over a coffee table, and whether it is done by writing a letter, in conversation, or by writing a book.

What we call *training and equipping the saints* is also a ministry of the Word, in which Christians are given not only the Bible's teaching on the Christian life and Christian ministry, but also practical training and feedback on their ministry.

What we call *counselling* is, or at least should be, a ministry of the Word, when, usually in the context of a private conversation, an individual is helped to see his or her position before God in the light of his words from the Bible, and how he or she might change to become a more godly person.

The *public reading of Scripture* is also a ministry of the Word, in which the truth of God for this generation is proclaimed to the congregation.

Another ministry of the Word is that of *choosing Bible readings.* Those who are committed to the use of a publicly produced lectionary, of course, need not worry about their theology of lectionary (that is, how to choose one Bible reading rather than another). But for those who exercise more personal initiative in choosing Bible readings for any occasion, the choice of a particular Bible reading is of course a profound exercise of the ministry of the Word. For the question will always be, 'Why choose this particular reading from God's Word rather than another?'

What we call *preaching* is a ministry of the Word. By 'preaching' we mean, as I have said, the public, formal monologue to the congregation. It is important to see the context of this particular ministry of the Word in the light of other ministries of the Word that occur within the congregation.

We have described preaching in Hoekstra's words as 'the administration of the Word in the assembled congregation of Christ'. We now need to change it, because 'the administration of the Word' includes not only preaching, but also the public reading of Scripture, a ministry of the Word of great importance ('Until I come, give attention to the public reading of scripture, to exhorting, to teaching', 1 Tim. 4:13; see also Col. 4:16 and Rev. 1:3), and also the selection of what is to be read. Our definition should therefore read: 'the explanation and application of the Word in the assembled congregation of Christ'.

It may seem heretical to suggest that preaching is not the sole focus of Christian ministry of the Word. We now look, therefore, at John Calvin and Richard Baxter, to examine their varied ministries of the Word.

John Calvin

This diversity of the ministry of the Word is demonstrated most clearly in the life and ministry of John Calvin. Calvin has a very high view of the ministry of the Word.

> But as God did not entrust the ancient folk to angels but raised up teachers from the earth truly to perform the angelic office, so also today it is his will to teach us through human means. As he was of old not content with the law alone, but added priests as interpreters from whose lips the people might ask its true meaning, so today he not only desires us to be attentive to its reading but also appoints instructors to help us by their effort. This is doubly useful. On the one hand, he provokes our obedience by a very good test when we hear his ministers speaking just as if he himself spoke. On the other hand, he also provides for our weakness in that he prefers to address us in human fashion through interpreters in order to draw us to himself, rather than to thunder at us and drive us away.[3]

We can describe Calvin's various ministries of the Word in the following four ways.

Calvin the writer. We have already noted the importance of writing in the ministry of the Word, in order to promote biblical faith not only in Geneva but also throughout his world of influence. We can divide his writings into the following categories.

First, he wrote *theology*. He is best known for the various editions of his

Institutes of the Christian Religion, but he also wrote theological treatises: for example, the *Genevan Confession* (1536), the *Catechism for the Church of Geneva* (1545), the short *Treatise on the Lord's Supper* (1541), and the *Confession of Faith Concerning the Eucharist* (1537). To these we can add his more controversial writings including his *Reply to Sadolet* (1539).[4]

Secondly, he wrote *documents of church order*. His articles *Concerning the Organization of the Church and of Worship at Geneva* (1537), *Draft Ecclesiastical Ordinances* (1541), and the *Ordinances for the Supervision of Churches in the Country* (1547), are examples of Calvin's ministry of the Word in promoting good order for the churches for which he had responsiblity.

Thirdly, he wrote *biblical commentaries*. These represent a great commitment to the ministry of the Word. Many of them originated from his public teaching and preaching in Geneva, but their written form can be seen as another formative expression of the ministry of the Word at the time of the Reformation.

Fourthly, Calvin wrote *letters*. This also reflects a ministry of the word. Jean-Daniel Benoit, in his chapter 'Calvin the Letter-Writer,'[5] describes the great extent of Calvin's letter-writing. He wrote to the most powerful political leaders of his world, including the kings of England, Denmark and Poland; the king and queen of Navarre; his fellow reformers in France, Switzerland, the Netherlands and England; prisoners and martyrs; and his friends. Benoit, quoting Calvin, points out that the Reformer himself saw his letter-writing as a ministry of the Word.

> He desired to lead souls in the right way which God has shown in his word. 'You know how the Scripture warns us to give us courage as we fight for the cause of the Son of God. Meditate on what you have seen and heard formally so that you may put it into practice. Everything that I can ever tell you will not help unless it is drawn from this well.' 'You really do not need my letters so much for what you hope to learn from me you can find much nearer to hand if you diligently read God's holy Word.'[6]

Calvin the public speaker. For the inhabitants of Geneva Calvin was primarily a public speaker. The church at Geneva engaged in a rigorous programme of education, of which the first example is that of preaching. The normal pattern of preaching in Geneva in Calvin's time was this: each Sunday began with a service and sermon at daybreak, continued with the catechism for the children at midday, and concluded with another sermon at three o'clock. Sermons were also fixed for Monday, Tuesday and Friday mornings until, in 1549, they increased to every day of the week. Calvin's practice was to preach twice each Sunday at St Pierre's and once every day on alternate weeks. On Sundays his method was to preach through the New Testament except for a few psalms on Sunday afternoons. His weekday sermons were almost always from the Old Testament.[7]

Of course, the sermons that Calvin preached not only were a *spoken* ministry of the Word but also became a *written* ministry of the Word, after the 'company of strangers' in 1549 arranged for his sermons to be taken down in shorthand, transcribed, printed and then published. But the sermons' initial purpose was the public declaration of the Word of God to the people of Geneva, and any account of Calvin's ministry of the Word must place great weight on his preaching ministry. (We shall study Calvin's preaching in chapter 6.)

In addition to preaching, Calvin gave lectures. The college which had been planned for so long was finally opened in 1559 and Calvin became one of the two theological professors with responsibility for the Old Testament. His lectures on the Old Testament were copied down and eventually published as part of his commentaries. As with his preaching, Calvin's spoken ministry of the Word in lecture form became a written ministry of the Word. The college served not only the people of Geneva but also students from all over Europe.[8] As P. J. Wilcox has shown, these lectures (expositions of books of the Bible) were at first given in a chapel in St Pierre's and later in the college. (This was not the Collège de Rive, for children, but the college for adults.) Here Calvin's audience was made up of members of the college, ministers and temporary residents in Geneva. Wilcox shows that the college was in fact a training-school or seminary for ministers of the Word, many of whom would return to their native countries (they were mostly from France) to evangelize and plant churches. He also points out that Calvin's lectures on the prophets have as a major focus the evangelistic mission of the church, in terms of the growing kingdom of Christ and the 'restoration' of the church. Calvin's lectures were his way of training ministers and missionaries to Europe. His contemporary, Viret, estimated that 1,000 people attended the lectures every day.[9]

In addition to sermons and lectures Calvin also frequently spoke at the weekly 'congregation'. This was held on Friday, when pastors from Geneva and the surrounding countryside met together for study of the Bible and mutual admonition.[10] Calvin's ministry in these weekly congregations, too, was transcribed and later published. Again, his spoken ministry became a written ministry.[11]

We should notice that Calvin's public spoken ministry included both the edification of the church at Geneva and also the public training of ministers and missionaries.

Church discipline. For Calvin the ministry of the Word meant not only forms of public teaching, preaching and writing, but also the implementation of a biblical style of church government and a biblical pattern of life among the people of Geneva. His work on the *Church Ordinances*, and his membership of the Consistory (which caused him and the Genevans so much trouble), were other aspects of his desire to be a servant of God's Word. Wendel claims: 'Calvin was clearly the moving spirit of the Consistory. To study the official documents is to find traces of his initiative almost everywhere. Everything had to contribute to making a saintly city of Geneva.'[12]

Ministry to individuals. To get a comprehensive view of Calvin's ministry of the Word it is important to see that he also engaged in what is now called pastoral work.

> He was a pastor, busied with the common run of pastoral duties. For example, glancing through the Annals of Geneva we find that on November 5th 1553 he married two couples in the Cathedral; that on December 10th of the same year he 'blessed a marriage and administered baptism at St. Pierre'. All in all . . . for the ten years 1550–1559 . . . he took about two hundred and seventy weddings and fifty baptisms. There seems to have been no regular house to house visiting by the pastors, but only visits to those who were sick or in some trouble. Calvin undertook this duty also.[13]

Parker quotes Calvin's account of the pastoral visiting programme during the plague that came to Geneva in 1542. Calvin wrote:

> The pestilence begins to rage here with greater violence . . . One of our colleagues had to be set apart for visiting the sick. Because Peter offered himself everyone readily agreed! If anything happens to him, I am afraid I must take the risk on myself since, as you say, we must not fail those who stand in more need of our ministry than any others . . . I do not see that any excuse will avail us if, through fear of infection, we are found wanting in the discharge of our duty where we are most needed.[14]

Calvin's contemporary, Colladon, describes Calvin's life and ministry as follows.

> Calvin for his part did not spare himself at all, working far beyond what his powers and regard for his health could stand. He preached commonly every day for one week in two. Every week he lectured three times in theology. He was at the *Consistoire* on the appointed day and made all the remonstrances. Every Friday at the Bible Study which we call the

Congrégation, what he added after the leader had made his *déclaration* was almost a lecture. He never failed in visiting the sick, in private warning and counsel, and the rest of the numberless matters arising out of the ordinary exercise of his ministry. But besides these ordinary tasks, he had great care for believers in France, both in teaching them and exhorting them and counselling them and consoling them by letters when they were being persecuted, and also interceding for them, or getting another to intercede when he thought he saw an opening. Yet all that did not prevent him from going on working at his special study and composing many splendid and useful books.[15]

Again, the point being made is the great diversity of Calvin's ministry of the Word. This was not accidental. It was part of Calvin's strategy of ministry, as we can see in the *Draft Ecclesiastical Ordinances* which Calvin drew up for Geneva in 1541. This illustrated a variety of ways in which the ministry of the Word of God is to be implemented.

There are four orders of office instituted by our Lord for the government of his church. First, pastors; then doctors [teachers]; next elders; and fourth deacons. Hence if we will have a church well ordered and maintained we ought to observe this form of government. As to the pastors, whom Scripture also sometimes calls elders and ministers, their office is to proclaim the Word of God, to instruct, admonish, exhort and censure, both in public and private, to administer the sacraments and to enjoin brotherly corrections along with the elders and colleagues . . .

The office of doctors is the instruction of the faithful in true doctrine in order that the purity of the gospel be not corrupted either by ignorance or evil opinions. As things are disposed today we will always include under this title aids and instructions for maintaining the doctrine of God and defending the church from injury by the fault of pastors and ministers. So to use a more intelligible word, we will call this the order of the schools. The degree nearest to the minister and most closely joined to the government of the church is the lecturer in theology, of which it would be good to have one in Old Testament and one in New Testament.

The office of elders is to have oversight of the life of everyone, to admonish amicably those whom they see to be erring or to be living a disordered life, and where it is required to enjoin fraternal corrections themselves and along with others.

The fourth order, that of deacons, consists in more practical ministries.[16]

As further evidence we may quote from the *Institutes*. When Calvin is writing about the pastoral task he says that 'the manner of teaching not only consists in public discourses, but also has to do with private admonitions'.[17] To complete Calvin's picture of the ministry of the Word in the congregation we should include his comment that 'it is clear that every member of the church is charged with the responsibility of public edification according to the measure of his grace, provided he perform it decently and in order'.[18]

Richard Baxter

The point I have been making is a simple but important one: there are more forms of the ministry of the Word than what we call preaching. It is a common assumption that the Reformed tradition of Christianity is committed to preaching. That is why it has been useful to look at the example of Calvin to see that both in theory and in practice Calvin's view of the ministry of the Word extended beyond preaching only. We can learn the same point from one of the most significant writers on the pastoral ministry, Richard Baxter.

J. I. Packer reminds us that on the title page of the original edition of Richard Baxter's *The Reformed Pastor*, 'the word *reformed* was printed in much larger type than any other, and one does not have to read far before discovering that for Baxter a "reformed" pastor was not one who campaigned for Calvinism but one whose ministry to his people as preacher, teacher, catechist and role model showed him to be, as we would say, "revived" or "renewed"'.[19]

In my edition of Baxter's *The Reformed Pastor*[20] the title page reads as follows:

Gildas Salvianus

The Reformed Pastor:

shewing
the nature of the pastoral work:
especially in private instruction and catechising: with an
open confession of our too open sins.
Prepared for
a day of humiliation kept at Worcester
December 4, 1655, by the ministers of that county, who
subscribed the agreement for catechising and personal
instruction, at their entrance upon that work

We might have expected *The Reformed Pastor* to defend the preaching office. In fact, Baxter promotes a rather different model of pastoral ministry. The whole book explains Paul's commission to the Ephesian elders in Acts 20 to feed the church of God. In true Puritan style Baxter describes the various groups of people who may be found in the flock of any one pastor, including the unconverted and the converted, those who are young and weak, those who are suffering particular pressure, those who are declining from their faith, those who are under great temptation, those who are disconsolate, and those who are strong in faith. What then of the content of the oversight? Baxter describes it as public preaching; the sacraments; public prayer, praise and benediction; and oversight of the members distinctly (by which he means pastoral work which is focused on individuals and families rather than on the congregation as a whole). He explains these elements as follows.

Of preaching he says:

> One part of our work, and that the most excellent, because it tendeth to work on many, is the public preaching of the word – a work that requireth greater skill, and especially greater life and zeal, than any of us bring to it. It is no small matter to stand up in the face of the congregation, and deliver a message of salvation or damnation, as from the living God, in the name of our Redeemer. It is no easy matter to speak so plain, that the ignorant may understand us; and so seriously, that the deadest heart may feel us; and so convincingly, that contradicting cavillers may be silenced.[21]

Of the sacraments he says: 'Another part of our pastoral work is to administer the holy mysteries, or seals of God's covenants – Baptism and the Lord's Supper.'[22]

'Another part of our work', he continues, 'is to guide our people, and to be as their mouth in the public prayers of the church, and the public praises of God; as also to bless them in the name of the Lord. This sacerdotal part of the work is not the least, nor is it to be so much thrust into a corner, as by many of us it is.'[23]

'Another part of the ministerial work, is to have a special care and oversight of each member of the flock.'[24] Baxter notes that exercising this special care and oversight of each member involves knowing them individually and personally, 'for if we know not the temperament or disease, we are likely to prove but unsuccessful physicians'.[25] Baxter also encourages his readers to use 'all the means we can to instruct the ignorant in the matters of their salvation: by our own most plain familiar words; by giving, or lending, or otherwise helping them to books that are fit for them; by persuading them to learn catechisms; and those that cannot read, to get help of their neighbours; and to persuade their neighbours to afford them help, who have best opportunities thereto.'[26]

This also involves giving advice to those who come to the minister with special issues of conscience. 'A minister is not only for public preaching but to be a known counsellor for their souls, as a lawyer is for their estates, and the physician for their bodies; so that each man that is in doubts and straits, should bring his case to him and desire resolution.'[27]

This personal and particular care is to focus on families as well as individuals. 'We must also have a special eye upon families, to see that they be well ordered, and the duties of each relation performed, – the life of religion, and the welfare and glory of Church and State, depending much on family government and duty. If we suffer the neglect of this, we undo all.'[28] For Baxter, the family as a pastoral unit was of key importance in reforming the parish. 'What are we like to do ourselves to the reforming of a congregation, if all the work be cast on us alone, and masters of families will let fall that necessary duty of their own, by which they are bound to help us? If any good be begun by the ministry in any soul in a family, a careless, prayerless, worldly family is almost sure to stifle it, or at least very much hinder it.'[29] J. I. Packer observes that the parish contained about 2,000 adults and about 800 homes. Baxter's policy was to spend an hour with each of seven family units invited to his home, that is seven hours altogether on Monday and Tuesday afternoons and evenings, and by this means have pastoral contact with nearly all the parish families once a year.[30] Packer also notes that in Baxter's pastoral ministry the family unit performed the function of modern cell groups or small groups.

It is interesting to notice Baxter's advice on how to minister to families:

i. Get certain information how each family is ordered, and how God is worshipped in them, that you may know how to proceed in your carefulness for their further good.

ii. Go now and then among them when they are like to be most at leisure, and ask the master of the family whether he pray with them or read the Scripture or what he doth?

iii. If you find any unable to pray in tolerable expressions through ignorance and disuse, persuade them to study their own wants, and get their hearts affected with them, and so go often to those neighbours who use to pray, that they may learn, and in the meantime persuade them to use a form of prayer other than none.

iv. See that they have some profitable, moving book (beside the Bible) in each family, and if they have not persuade them to buy some of small price and great use . . .

v. By all means persuade them to procure all their children to learn to read English.

vi. Direct them how to spend the Lord's Day, how to dispatch their worldly business so as to prevent incumbrances and distractions; and when they have been at the assembly how to spend the time in their families . . . Especially persuade them to these two things: if they cannot repeat the sermon, or otherwise spend the time profitably at home, that they take their family with them and go to some godly neighbour that spends it better, that by joining with them they may have the better help. That the master of the family will every Lord's Day at night, cause all his family to repeat the catechism to him, and give some account of what they have learned in public that day.

vii. If there be any in the family that are known to be unruly, give the ruler a special charge concerning them, and make them understand what a sin it is to connive at and tolerate them.[31]

Baxter later looked back on his own ministry and saw the following results of his pastoral work.

The congregation was usually full, so that we were fain to build five galleries after my coming thither . . . The church would have held about a thousand without the galleries. Our private Meetings were also full. On the Lord's Days there was no disorder to be seen in the Streets, but you might hear a hundred Families singing Psalms and repeating Sermons as you pass through the Streets. In a word, when I came thither first, there was not past one Family in a Street that worshipped God and called on His Name, and when I came away there were some Streets where there was not one Family in the side of the Street that did not so; and that did not by professing serious Godliness give us hopes of their sincerity.[32]

Packer gives a full picture of Baxter's ministries of the Word:

In his regular sermons (one each Sunday and Thursday, each lasting an hour) he taught basic Christianity . . . In addition he held a weekly pastors' forum for discussion and prayer; he distributed Bibles and Christian books . . . he taught individuals through personal counselling and catechising . . . to upgrade the practice of personal catechising from a preliminary discipline for children to a permanent ingredient in evangelism and pastoral care for all ages was Baxter's main contribution to the development of Puritan ideals for the ministry; and it was his concern for catechising that brought *The Reformed Pastor* to birth.[33]

My aim in citing these various passages is not to denigrate preaching but to show that a wider view of the ministry of the Word is appropriate and that preaching plays its proper role within the context of this wider ministry.

What then is preaching?

We have described preaching as 'the explanation and application of the Word in the assembled congregation of Christ', and it is important to see that this description indicates both the strengths and weaknesses of preaching.

Preaching is of course addressed to the congregation. The great advantage of this is that it provides an opportunity to address the believers assembled as the body of Christ. Preaching is essentially a corporate activity and its most useful aim is corporate edification. In this, preaching reflects the main burden of the message of the Bible, in which most of the books are directed not to individuals or to leaders but to the people of God. This is most clearly seen in Paul's epistles, most of which are addressed to churches rather than to individuals or even to leaders of the churches. This means that the sermon's focus of address is most appropriately not individuals and their needs but the needs of the congregation as a whole. This is not to say that individuals may not be greatly helped or encouraged by the sermon, but its primary aim is the welfare, obedience, holiness, godliness and good working of the congregation. Paul describes this corporate maturing and edification in Ephesians 4:11–13:

> The gifts he gave were that some would be apostles, some prophets, some evangelists, some pastors and teachers, to equip the saints for the work of ministry, for building up the body of Christ, until all of us come to the unity of the faith and of the knowledge of the Son of God, to maturity, to the measure of the full stature of Christ.

It is important to emphasize this, for our current Protestant preoccupation is with the application of the Bible to the individual. 'What is the Bible saying to me?' The Bible is treated as if it were God's message to the individual. This preoccupation with personal and individual application probably begins when we do one-to-one evangelism; it is fuelled by Enlightenment teaching about the autonomy of the individual, and by our society's existentialist concern for personal growth and development; and it is facilitated by the availability of Bibles for individuals to own and read on their own. But the Bible's main address is to the community of faith, the church. If this is what the Bible is doing, then preaching that is true to the Bible will follow its lead, and aim for corporate edification, unity, maturity and growth, as described in Ephesians 4.

This corporate audience of the Word means that we should again modify our definition of preaching. At its last sighting, it read: 'the explanation and application of the Word in the assembled congregation of Christ'. But preaching not only takes place *in* the congregation, it is addressed *to* the congregation. And since I think it is always useful to add an aim or purpose to a definition, why not include those great aims from Ephesians 4? Our definition now reads: 'the explanation and application of the Word to the congregation of Christ in order to produce corporate preparation for service, unity of faith, maturity, growth and upbuilding'.

Moreover, Sunday-by-Sunday preaching is not the only way to address the edification of individuals. The main purpose of the Sunday sermon is the edification of the body. While individuals may be edified in so far as they are members of the congregation, there may well be other areas in which they need correction and training in righteousness which they will not obtain through the Sunday sermon, because by its very nature it is generalist in its application. Of course individuals will be edified as the congregation is edified, but each individual also needs personal challenge and encouragement in the obedience of faith.

Preaching, in our definition, is a public presentation of the truth. It is mostly done in the context in which anybody may come and hear. The good thing about this is that it reflects the public nature of God's revelation, and that it is freely accessible to anybody who chooses to attend and hear the explanation of the gospel and the application of God's Word to the lives of human beings today. The fact that it is a public occasion, however, means that it is an inappropriate context for personal rebuke of individuals whose lives may be a scandalous betrayal of the Christian faith. Those clergy who see preaching as the sole valid expression of ministry of the Word are forced to give up personal and individual rebuke and exhortation, or to administer it in the form of a public rebuke addressed to individuals in the congregation (which is inappropriate), or to rebuke the congregation for the sins of a few individuals (which is ineffective).

There is a place for public rebuke of individuals (Mt. 18:15–17; 1 Tim. 5:20), but it should be done openly, and not disguised as a general rebuke of the congregation. Disguising a personal rebuke in this way will not help the one who has sinned, and will harm the congregation.

Preaching is a formal monologue. The advantage of the formal monologue, the well-prepared sermon, is that the preacher has the opportunity in the preceding week to study the Word of God and to uncover the riches of its meaning, and then to bring it to the congregation. The disadvantage of this form of the ministry of the Word is that it does not allow scope for interaction between the preacher and the congregation. There is no room for questions or disagreement, and it does not allow the preacher to assess the response of the members of the congregation. A person who engages in the public ministry of preaching with no other contact with the congregation has little idea, in a polite society, whether the congregation thinks that what he is saying is rubbish or pure gold.

Preaching is our Word ministry to 'the assembled congregation of Christ'. This is central to our ministry. But we must also convert unbelievers, train people in ministry skills, and disciple and counsel individuals with the Word of God.

Let me state again that I am not opposed to preaching; indeed, I believe it is the central part of our ministry of the Word. But I think it is important to do justice to all the ministries of the Word and not to make preaching carry a burden which it is unable to bear.

Different models of ministries of the Word

To clarify the point I am making, we shall look at some examples of pastoral ministry and notice the strengths and weaknesses of various pastoral styles.

Pastor A is very committed to preaching as the ministry of the Word, and regards any other form as a distraction. He spends Monday to Thursday locked in his study preparing his sermon, and a considerable part of Sunday preaching it. His congregation is highly blessed in that they have a preacher who grapples seriously with the message of the Bible and produces a sermon which not only conveys the true message of the section of God's Word which is being preached, but also places that truth in the context of God's whole revelation in Jesus Christ. His congregation knows that he is a preacher who loves God's Word and is committed to its proclamation, and they should be thankful for that.

Yet there are some long-term disadvantages in this style of ministry. It may result in a congregation whose members are highly rebellious against God's Word. They accept it passively Sunday by Sunday, but it is bearing no fruit in their lives. Longer sermons will not solve this problem. Or it may be that the members of the congregation are enthusiastic listeners who have grasped the idea that the model Christian is the one who sits quietly and listens to sermons. The weakness in such a congregation is that they do not receive personal encouragement in their Christian lives and are not trained in Christian ministry.

Pastor B regards himself as no great preacher. His gift is applying the Word of God to individuals, and his time in his study is spent talking to members of the congregation about their Christian lives and encouraging them in godliness. When he is not in his study he is out visiting, engaged in the same kind of ministry. The advantage of this form of ministry is of course that he has a church full of godly people whose lives are conformed to the biblical pattern of obedience and whose Christian maturity is evident to all.

The disadvantage of this pattern of ministry is that while individuals may be edified, the congregation as a whole is not built up in maturity of faith, and this will have a dissipating effect on its energies. If no gospel strategy or training in ministry is being implemented, the people may be holy, but they will be frustrated because their congregation is not succeeding in evangelism or even attempting to engage in it, nor are they being taught how to encourage others in the faith.

Pastor C is a great preacher and biblical counsellor. He is never happier than when standing or sitting with Bible in hand and applying it either to the congregation or to individuals. But Pastor C is no strategist and is not engaged in a careful programme of implementing biblical policies and strategies for the life of his congregation. This provides the congregation with a great dilemnma. They are being encouraged and taught how to live and how to function as the people of God, but they see that the life of their congregation does not reflect these priorities because no-one has suggested how they might be implemented. The congregation and its members are well taught but very frustrated.

Pastor D is very committed to edification, and in every way that he can he will grasp hold of Christians to edify them and help them to grow in the faith. But he is so committed to edification that he has no time for evangelism. He is always addressing the congregation and its members, but does not know any unbelievers and has no effective strategy for meeting them or sharing the gospel with them. He has a congregation whose members are ultimately over-edified, and this edification may well turn sour if they do not receive the encouragement of seeing people converted and the enthusiasm of new believers. A congregation marked by edification but no evangelism will eventually become middle-aged and sour.

Pastor E is committed to edification, but has no strategy for training and equipping the saints. In his public preaching he is always telling his people that they ought to read the Bible for themselves, that they ought to evangelize, that they ought to be engaged in Christian ministry in the congregation, that they ought to be teachers of the faith, that they ought to be passing on their faith to their children, and that they ought to be effective leaders in the church. But he has no strategy for training or equipping his people for any of these ministries. The result is that the people will eventually grow restive and frustrated because they are continually being told to minister but are never trained to do it.

This pastor of course needs to continue his ministry of edification, but should also engage in some practical training and equipping, demonstrating to people by personal example how they should exercise these various ministries, giving them practical ways to begin their ministries so they can gain some confidence in them, providing feedback, and encouraging them to see ways forward in expanding them.

Pastor F is very committed to the public ministry of rebuke and correction and exhortation. He enjoys the public ministry partly because he dislikes personal interaction or confrontation with members of his congregation. He feels more secure in the pulpit than he does in someone's living-room. His congregation knows all about godliness, but there are certain key members whose lives are a scandal in terms of the Christian faith, and this includes some of the leaders. But because the pastor does not have the personal integrity to confront them with their sin individually, and perhaps because he does not view this as a legitimate ministry of the Word, he fails in his pastoral responsibility. Sinners remain unrebuked and the rest of the congregation grow more frustrated as they are castigated each week for the sins of others.

Pastor G has a strong view of edification and the need to preach the Bible. He works in a congregation where there is no set lectionary and so he is free to choose his own readings and thus the subjects of his sermons. Because he has never understood that the ministry of the Word involves selecting the public readings and planning the preaching programme, he is caught in a treadmill of preaching through the epistles year in and year out, and rarely ventures beyond the safety of St Paul. He cannot be said to be making full use of the words of God that are addressed to his congregation, and (though he does not realize it) he is in fact precluding his people from hearing God's words that have been addressed to them through the Old Testament and the gospels.

Pastor H has gone to a new congregation in which, as far as he can see, the leaders and most of the people are seriously deficient in Christian understanding and belief. His remedy is to preach stirring and challenging sermons. This will certainly produce the results he expects over the long term, but he would achieve his purpose sooner if he also offered to spend time in one-to-one discipling with the key leaders of the church, to convince them not only of the gospel and its significance for their lives but also of its priority in the life of the congregation. If they are not responsive, he should go out and convert and train new believers who will, in time, become the new leaders of the church.

In summary, then, an effective pastoral ministry will include not only preaching but also other ministries of the Word. As we have seen, both Calvin and Baxter were concerned to be ministers of the Word in many areas. This included public teaching and preaching, the forming of the life of the congregation in conformity to the Bible, the training of others in the ministry of the Word, private exhortation and encouragement, the production of Christian literature and its dissemination among the people, and the evangelization of unbelievers. Those of us who are committed to preaching need to be committed to a wider ministry of the Word as well. We need to see preaching as part of that ministry of the Word. Otherwise we shall try to make preaching do what it cannot easily achieve. Not only will God's people suffer because they do not receive other ministries of the Word, but our preaching will suffer as we force it into an alien mould. Our ministry may be pulpit-centred, but it should not be pulpit-restricted, for such a ministry of the Word will suffer severe limitations.

Our main subject, however, is preaching, which we have defined as 'the explanation and application of the Word to the congregation of Christ, in order to produce corporate preparation for service, unity of faith, maturity, growth and upbuilding'. With this understanding in mind we can now study the New Testament evidence.

New Testament evidence

When we turn to the New Testament to find out what it says about preaching we need to tread carefully. The New Testament does not tackle in great detail the function of what we call 'preaching', or 'sermons'; instead, it describes many different ministries of the Word. We can of course apply some of this material to our preaching. This means that a careful 'word study' approach may provide a way in to the subject, but will not give us all we need. A more wide-ranging and theological approach shows us that we can learn a great deal from the Bible about preaching, and that the Bible is most concerned about the ministry of the Word. For example, G. Friedrich in Kittel's *Theological Dictionary of the New Testament*[34] claims that the New Testament uses thirty-three verbs to express the activity of preaching. A more helpful way of viewing this is to say that the New Testament uses thirty-three verbs to describe a great variety of forms of ministry of the Word,[35] and these connect in various ways with our concept of preachng.

Because the New Testament does not compartmentalize its material on the ministry of the Word, we can see clearly how preaching fits into its more general pattern. What writers on preaching usually do is to look at a few key terms and use those to explain what preaching is.[36] To uncover the insights of the New Testament on preaching we shall examine its words and images; its model sermons; the epistles as examples of ministry of the Word; Paul as a model preacher; and Paul's teaching on the ministry of the Word.

New Testament words and images

While there is something artificial about looking at words separated from their context, it can be a useful way of surveying the extent of the material. If we take the 'ministry of the Word' verbs in the New

Testament, we can categorize the wide range as follows:

Words of information: teach, instruct, point out, make known, remind.

Words of declaration: preach, proclaim, cry out, testify, bear witness, declare, write, read, pass on, set forth.

Words of exhortation: call, denounce, warn, rebuke, command, give judgment, encourage, appeal, urge, ask.

Words of persuasion: explain, make clear, prove, guard, debate, contend, refute, reason, persuade, convince, insist, defend, confirm, stress.

Words of conversation: say, speak, talk, answer, reply, give answer.

Only a few of the words have to do with providing or passing on information. A merely didactic form of the ministry of the Word is inadequate. A high number of the words have to do with exhortation and persuasion, which have as their purpose a response within the hearers. We might also notice that the ministry of the Word can be continued in the context of ordinary conversation.

With regard to the content of the message which is communicated, the following terms are used: the preaching, the teaching, the word of encouragement, the word of God, the word of the Lord, the good news, the word of Christ, the gospel, the gospel of God, the whole counsel of God, the message, the words about Jesus Christ, the kingdom, the word of life, the truth, his commands, the deposit, the pattern, the faith, the Scriptures, the mystery of Christ, the truth of the gospel, Christ, Christ crucified, Jesus Christ as Lord, the new covenant. The New Testament uses a variety of images to describe the ministry of the Word: sowing the seed, treading out the grain, the harvest, planting the seed, watering the seed, providing milk, providing solid food, laying a foundation, being a father, work, giving birth, the fight, demolishing, making captive, tearing down, building up. The point of these images is that the ministry of the Word is exercised to some purpose. It is not mere teaching; it is teaching which achieves the purpose of God in changing people's lives.

Model sermons

One of the purposes of the New Testament writers is to provide us with a model ministry of the Word. In Luke and Acts, as we have seen, Luke has a strong concentration on the ministry of the Word. At the start of his ministry we read, 'Then Jesus, filled with the power of the Spirit, returned to Galilee, and a report about him spread through the surrounding country. He began to teach in their synagogues and was praised by everyone' (Lk. 4:14). The teaching ministry of Jesus is seen as a key to his whole ministry. This introduction is followed by Luke's account of Jesus' sermon at Nazareth on the Sabbath day in Luke 4:16–28. Here Jesus bases his teaching on the Old Testament, and points to the fulfilment of the Scripture in his address to his hearers. An expansion of this view of the ministry of the Word is found in Luke 24, where Jesus not only explains Isaiah, but also 'beginning with Moses and all the prophets, he interpreted to them the things about himself in all the scriptures' (24:27). The function of the teacher of the Bible in explaining the Old Testament in terms of its fulfilment in Jesus Christ is a favourite theme of Luke. He further describes the activity of Jesus in this study as opening the Scriptures (24:32) and then opening their minds (24:45). The main outline of the sermon and of Luke's theology of the ministry of the Word (the foundation of the ministry of the Word in the Old Testament and its fulfilment in Jesus Christ) is repeated later. 'He said to them, "These are my words that I spoke to you while I was still with you – that everything written about me in the law of Moses, the prophets, and the psalms must be fulfilled"' (24:44). 'He said to them. "Thus it is written, that the Messiah is to suffer and to rise from the dead on the third day, and that repentance and forgiveness of sins is to be proclaimed in his name to all nations, beginning from Jerusalem. You are witnesses of these things' (24:46–48).

Luke, like the other evangelists, describes Jesus as a rabbi or teacher, and part of the function of Luke's description of Jesus' teaching ministry is to provide a model for Christian teachers and preachers. We have noted two elements of Jesus' teaching: his use of the Old Testament and his theme of fulfilment and application. Within the book of Acts, the first Christian sermon is obviously of great importance not only as an explanation of the beginning of Christian ministry at Pentecost, but also as an example of the ministry of the Word with which Luke is so concerned. It has the following elements:

The introduction (Acts 2:14–21). Peter begins with the issue which has brought the crowd together: that is, people from many nations hearing the wonders of God in their own language (2:11). He points out that what the people were naturally assuming was not correct; the disciples were not drunk, and in fact the event is explained by the prophecy in Joel 2.

The main body of the sermon is found in verses 22–36, where Peter turns the occasion for good by moving away from the quotation from Joel to provide some information about the life and ministry of Jesus of Nazareth. He does this by explaining two passages from the Psalms, 16:8–11 and 110:1. The purpose is not merely to inform his hearers about salvation history but also to demonstrate their involvement in it: 'Therefore let the entire house of Israel know with certainty that God has made him both Lord and Messiah, this Jesus whom you crucified' (2:36).

In the third section of the sermon Peter gives *practical application* of the central part of his message, encouraging his hearers to action: 'Repent, and be baptized every one of you in the name of Jesus Christ so that your sins will be forgiven; and you will receive the gift of the Holy Spirit' (Acts 2:38). He also encourages them to this response by pointing them to

God's promise, 'for the promise is for you, for your children, and for all who are far away, everyone whom the Lord our God calls to him' (2:39).

Peter's ministry of the Word does not end with a mere declaration of the truth or with information about the kind of response that is appropriate. 'He testified with many other arguments and exhorted them, saying, "Save yourselves from this corrupt generation"' (2:40). Peter's ministry of the Word includes an *exegesis* of the Old Testament (Joel and Psalms), an *application* to his hearers, and also an *appeal* encouraging them to act in response to the Word of God which they have heard preached.

This pattern continues in the account of Paul's ministry with which Luke finishes the book of Acts. 'From morning until evening [Paul] explained the matter to them, testifying to the kingdom of God and trying to convince them about Jesus both from the law of Moses and from the prophets' (28:23). Luke summarizes Paul's ministry with these words: 'He lived there for two whole years at his own expense and welcomed all who came to him, proclaiming the kingdom of God or teaching about the Lord Jesus Christ with all boldness and without hindrance' (28:30–31). We should understand that to proclaim the kingdom of God or to teach about the Lord Jesus Christ is to explain the Scriptures of the Old Testament, apply them to the hearers, and encourage them to a response of repentance.[37]

From our study of New Testament words, then, we have found that preaching should include information, declaration, exhortation, application and persuasion; and from images of ministry that preaching should be productive. In models of sermons in Luke and Acts we have found that preaching should include explanation or exegesis, application and appeal.

New Testament epistles as models

It is a matter of considerable debate among New Testament scholars whether or not preaching and sermons lie closely behind New Testament documents, both gospels and epistles. This is not the place to discuss the general issue, but we can choose one New Testament epistle which does claim to be a form of ministry of the Word. The epistle to the Hebrews ends with these words: 'I appeal to you . . . to bear with my word of exhortation, for I have written to you briefly' (13:22). When the writer uses the words *urge* (*parakaleō*) and *exhortation* (*paraklēsis*) he is employing the common language of the verbal ministry of the Word, often described as an exhortation or in terms of the activity of exhorting. David Peterson illustrates this key ministry of the Word. He writes:

> *Paraklēsis* practiced by Paul involved the proclamation of the mighty acts of God in Christ, often with some exposition of the O.T., and a drawing out of the practical implications for the

audience in question – believers or unbelievers (*cf.* Acts 13:15–41). The terminology itself suggests that the activity had a summons to decision or an encouragement to persevere in the Christian way. Although systematic teaching was clearly involved, the address is not simply to the intellect but also to the affections and the will.[38]

My suggestion is that Hebrews is an example of the common ministry of exhortation in New Testament times which may have been either spoken or written. As Richard Longenecker[39] notes, Hebrews is based on five Old Testament portions: (1) verses from the Psalms, 2 Samuel 7 and Deuteronomy 32; (2) Psalm 8:4–6; (3) Psalm 95:7–11; (4) Psalm 110:4; and (5) Jeremiah 31:31–34. We find that the ingredients in New Testament preaching which we have already discovered in Acts 2 are here present in Hebrews, namely an explanation of Old Testament texts in terms of their Christian fulfilment, their application to the people who are hearing or reading the message and strong encouragement to them to take action in response to the message.

While one of the most obvious features of the epistle to the Hebrews is its explanation of the Old Testament, another feature of equal importance is the application and exhortation to those who are hearing or reading the message.

> We must pay greater attention to what *we* have heard, so that *we* do not drift away from it. (2:1)

> Since, then, *we have* a great high priest who has passed through the heavens, Jesus, the Son of God, *let us* hold fast to our confession. (4:14)

> Therefore, my friends, *since we have* confidence to enter the sanctuary by the blood of Jesus, by the new and living way that he opened for us through the curtain, (that is, through his flesh), and *since we have* a great priest over the house of God, *let us* approach with a true heart in full assurance of faith . . . *let us* consider how to provoke one another to love and good deeds, not neglecting to meet together, as is the habit of some, but encouraging one another – and all the more as you see the Day approaching. (10:19–25)

Hebrews provides a fine example of New Testament exhortation. The only debatable feature is that the writer describes it as brief!

Paul as a model preacher

In his own description of his ministry, Paul depicts not only his unique role as the apostle to the Gentiles but also the more general Christian ministry of the Word.[40] This is particularly evident in 1 and 2 Corinthians. It is not always easy to discover what Paul means when he uses 'we' and 'us', but when he talks about his Christian ministry in these two epistles he seems to be using it as an example of godly forms of gospel ministry in contrast to that of his opponents. For instance, he writes: 'Jews demand signs and Greeks desire wisdom, but we proclaim Christ crucified: a stumbling-block to Jews and foolishness to Gentiles, but to those who are the called, both Jews and Greeks, Christ the power of God and the wisdom of God' (1 Cor. 1:22–24). The 'we' who proclaim Christ are not only Paul and Sosthenes but also all who are committed to Paul's gospel. Similarly, Paul says: 'My speech and my proclamation were not with plausible words of wisdom, but with a demonstration of the Spirit and of power' (2:4). He is not only explaining his own ministry but also giving a model of Christian ministry, in contrast to his opponents who appear to be worldly wise in their preaching.

Later in 1 Corinthians Paul talks about his own ministry and the ministry of Apollos, and he again contrasts godly forms and models of gospel ministry with understandings of what takes place. 'What then is Apollos? What is Paul? Servants through whom you came to believe, as the Lord has assigned to each. I planted, Apollos watered, but God gave the growth. So neither the one who plants nor the one who waters is anything, but only God who gives the growth' (3:5–7). Again Paul generalizes from a description of his own ministry and encourages others to take note of his example. His description of his own ministry provides the basis for an exhortation to others. 'According to the grace of God given to me, like a skilled master builder I laid a foundation, and someone else is building on it. Each builder must choose with care how to build on it' (3:10).

Paul also describes himself and his friends as 'servants of Christ and stewards of God's mysteries' (4:1), and again applies this to his hearers: 'I have applied all this to Apollos and myself for your benefit, brothers and sisters, so that you may learn through us the meaning of the saying, "Nothing beyond what is written", so that none of you will be puffed up in favour of one against another' (4:6). Paul himself is a model to the Corinthians not only in their life but also in their ministry: 'though you have ten thousand guardians in Christ, you do not have many fathers. Indeed, in Christ Jesus I became your father through the gospel. I appeal to you, then, be imitators of me' (4:15–16).

Again, when discussing the subject of food offered to idols, Paul responds to the Corinthians' question in terms of his own apostleship, and his policy of using his freedom for the benefit of others (9:14, 22). His practice is an example not only of life but of ministry. 'So whether you eat or drink, or whatever you do, do everything for the glory of God . . . I try to please everyone in everything I do, not seeking my own advantage, but that of many, so that they may be saved. Be imitators of me, as I am of Christ' (10:31 – 11:1).

In 2 Corinthians also, Paul paints a picture of his own ministry as an example for other Christian ministers. In saying that God 'has made us competent to be ministers of a new covenant' (3:6), Paul is describing not only his own ministry as an apostle but also that of all who join with him in preaching the apostolic gospel. He repeatedly outlines the style of his ministry, not only to explain to the Corinthians why they ought to believe the gospel that he has given them, but also to encourage them to exercise a comparable ministry.

> We are not peddlers of God's word like so many, but in Christ we speak as persons of sincerity, as persons sent from God. (2:17)

> Therefore, since it is by God's mercy that we are engaged this ministry, we do not lose heart. We have renounced the shameful things that one hides; we refuse to practise cunning or to falsify God's word; but by the open statement of truth we commend ourselves to the conscience of everyone in the sight of God. (4:1–2)

Like Paul's ministry, theirs should honour God.

Paul speaks of Christian ministry in terms of being a minister of the new covenant and of the reconciliation which God has achieved in Christ. He is concerned not only with the content of ministry but also with its style:

> As servants of God we have commended ourselves in every way: through great endurance, through afflictions, hardships, calamities, beatings, imprisonments, riots, labours, sleepless nights, hunger; by purity, knowledge, patience, kindness, holiness of spirit, genuine love, truthful speech, and the power of God; with the weapons of righteousness for the right hand and for the left; in honour and dishonour, in ill repute and good repute. We are treated as impostors and yet are true; as unknown, and yet are well known; as dying, and see – we are alive; as punished, and yet not killed; as sorrowful, yet always rejoicing; as poor, yet making many rich; as having nothing, and yet possessing everything. (6:4–10)

The style of Paul's ministry is further illustrated by his defence of it against the criticisms of those engaged in different forms of ministry and who preach different gospels. Paul describes his ministry in these terms:

> Indeed, we live as human beings, but we do not wage war according to human standards; for the weapons of our warfare are not merely human, but they have divine power to destroy strongholds. We destroy arguments and every proud obstacle raised up against the knowledge of God, and we take every thought captive to obey Christ. (10:3–5)

The purpose of Paul's self-revelation, then, is not only to give the Corinthians a clear idea of the authenticity of his own gospel ministry, but also to provide them with a model of Christian living and Christian ministry (see also 2 Cor. 11:21–29). He does this not so much by setting examples of techniques of preaching but by explaining the nature, authority and truth of his gospel and the style of his ministry, and the suffering that results from his gospel aims.

Paul provides a model of Christian ministry because of his particular role in salvation history. He describes himself as

> Paul, a servant of God and an apostle of Jesus Christ, for the sake of the faith of God's elect and the knowledge of truth that is in accordance with godliness, in the hope of eternal life that God, who never lies, promised before the ages began – in due time he revealed his word through the proclamation with which I have been entrusted by the command of God our Saviour. (Tit. 1:1–3)

Paul sets forth a model for Christian ministry in every age. He explicitly models gospel ministry in content and style; this includes his message of Christ crucified, his trust in God and in the day of Christ for the vindication of his ministry, ministering for the benefit of others and to the glory of God, not distorting the message but explaining it plainly, and commending his ministry and his gospel by his integrity and his suffering.

Paul's teaching on ministry of the Word

As we saw in chapter 3, it is in the pastoral epistles (1 and 2 Timothy and Titus) that we get some of the clearest teaching on post-apostolic ministry of the Word. They portray that form of ministry which should prevail in our churches today. Paul's counsel regarding elders is in part conveyed by specific instructions. But the qualities of life and ministry required of those elders are also depicted in Paul's understanding of his own ministry as a herald, apostle and teacher of the true faith to the Gentiles (1 Tim. 2:7), and in his instructions to Timothy and Titus, Paul's delegates, about their own life and ministry.

Paul's central concern in these letters is to instruct people in living as members of God's household, the church of the living God, which is called to be the pillar and bulwark of the truth (1 Tim. 3:15). The means that God has provided to continue the ministry of the Word is the overseer or elder (1 Tim. 3:1–13); without these teaching elders, a congregation is incomplete (Tit. 1:5). These are Paul's requirements and priorities for the nature of the local church and its ministry: as we have seen in chapter 3, these priorities should be ours as well.

Paul wants elders appointed who are of sound moral character and have demonstrated ability in leadership, management, and personal relationships (1 Tim. 3:1-7; Tit. 1:5–9). The requirement that elders should manage their households well (1 Tim. 3:4–5) will include the family trade as well as domestic family life. Elders or overseers must be of such a character that even outsiders recognize their qualities, and they must not be recent converts (1 Tim. 3:6–7). Elders will also be distinguished by their theological clarity, and their ability to teach the truth and reprove error (Tit. 1:9). This theological clarity will derive from the study of the Scriptures, as in the case of Timothy himself (2 Tim. 3:15), and will result in wisdom about the way of salvation through faith in Jesus Christ, and in being equipped for every good work (2 Tim. 3:15–16). Commitment to the truth is also expressed by loyalty to Paul and his teaching – Paul's pattern of sound teaching, the good deposit of faith (Tim. 1:13–14).

The characteristics of the ministry engaged in by elders or overseers include the public reading of Scripture, exhorting and teaching (1 Tim. 4:13; 5:17), encouragement of sound doctrine and the public refutation of those who oppose it (Tit. 1:9). As was the case for Timothy and Titus themselves, no doubt suffering will be part of the elders' experience (2 Tim. 1:8–12; 2:1–7; 3:10–13). Similarly, their style of ministry will be based on that of Paul, Timothy and Titus, and not on that of the false teachers (1 Tim. 1:6–7; 6:3–10; 2 Tim. 2:22 – 3:9, Tit. 1:10–16; 3:9–11).

One of the characteristic expressions found in the pastorals is the description of doctrine or words as 'sound' (*hygiainō*).

> Whatever else is contrary to the *sound* teaching . . . If anyone teaches otherwise and does not agree with the *sound* words of our Lord Christ and the teaching that is in accordance with godliness . . . Hold to the standard of *sound* teaching that you heard from me, in the faith and love that are in Christ Jesus . . . For the time is coming when people will not put up with *sound* doctrine . . . [A bishop] must have a firm grasp of the word that is trustworthy in accordance with the teaching, so that he may be able both to preach with *sound* doctrine and to refute those who contradict it . . . For this reason rebuke them sharply, so that they may become *sound* in the faith . . . teach what is consistent with *sound*

doctrine. Tell the older men to be temperate, serious, prudent, and *sound* in faith, in love, and in endurance.

(1 Tim. 1:10; 6:3; 2 Tim. 1:13; 4:3; Tit. 1:9; 13; 2:1–2)

In our English tradition we usually regard the word 'sound' as meaning 'correct' or 'orthodox' In the pastorals, however, the word has more obvious pastoral implications. To be sound is to be healthy; healthy doctrine is doctrine which is not only true but also productive of godliness. Sound doctrine is healthy teaching; that is, it changes peoples' lives.

We began this chapter by reflecting on the variety of forms of the ministry of the Word in the New Testament. We also saw this variety expressed in the models of ministry of John Calvin and Richard Baxter. Our aim was to show that preaching is not the only ministry of the Word. To appreciate this will help us not to have too high an expectation of preaching (that it will achieve everything that the Word is meant to do). It also meant that we were in a better position to survey the New Testament evidence, and not to interpret it too narrowly as preaching alone rather than in terms of the many different ministries of the Word.

With all this in mind we then studied the distinctive features of what we call 'preaching', 'the explanation and application of the Word to the congregation of Christ, in order to produce corporate preparation for service, unity of faith, maturity, growth and upbuilding'. We noted its particular characteristic of promoting corporate edification. We also noted what preaching will not easily or usually achieve. I argued for a ministry that is pulpit-centred, but not pulpit-restricted.

We went on to survey the New Testament evidence about the ministry of the Word which we can relate to preaching, including words and images of preaching, model sermons, and model preaching. We also studied some of the New Testament teaching about the ministries of the Word which we can apply to preaching today.

Notes

1. Anthony Hoekstra, quoted in Sidney Greidanus, *Sola Scriptura: Preaching Historical Texts* (Toronto: Wedge, 1970), p. 7.

2. Phillips Brooks, *Lectures on Preaching* (London: Allenson, n. d.), p. 5.

3. Calvin, *Institutes* IV.i.5. See also T. H. L. Parker, *Calvin's Preaching* (Edinburgh: T. and T. Clark, 1992), Part 1.

4. See, *e.g.*, Calvin's *Theological Treatises*, in the Library of Christian Classics, vol. 22, ed. J. K. S. Reid (London: SCM, 1954).

5. Jean–Daniel Benoît, 'Calvin the Letter–Writer', in G. E. Duffield (ed.), *John Calvin*, Courtenay Studies in Reformation Theology (Abingdon: Sutton Courtenay Press, 1970), pp. 67–101.

6. *Ibid.*, p. 93.

7. T. H. L. Parker, *Portrait of Calvin* (London: SCM, 1954), p. 82.

8. T. H. L. Parker, *John Calvin* (London: J. M. Dent, 1975), pp. 128–129.

9. See 'The Audience of Calvin's Lectures', in P. J. Wilcox, *Restoration, Reformation and the Progress of the Kingdom of Christ: Evangelization in the Thought and Practice of John Calvin 1555–1564* (unpublished Oxford DPhil thesis, 1993), pp. 58–65.

10. Parker, *John Calvin*, p. 89.

11. T. H. L. Parker, 'Calvin the Biblical Expositor', in Duffield (ed.), *John Calvin*, pp. 187–189.

12. François Wendel, *Calvin* (Eng. trans. London: Collins, 1965), p. 85.

13. Parker, *Portrait of Calvin*, pp. 80–81.

14. *Ibid.*, p. 81.

15. Quoted in Parker, *Calvin's Preaching*, pp. 62–63.

16. Calvin, *Theological Treatises*, pp. 58ff.

17. Calvin, *Institutes* IV.iii.6, p. 1059.

18. *Ibid.*, IV.i.12, p. 1026.

19. J. I. Packer, *A Quest for Godliness: The Puritan Vision of the Christian Life* (Wheaton: Crossway, 1990) = *Among God's Giants: The Puritan Vision of the Christian Life* (Eastbourne: Kingsway, 1991), p. 30.

20. Richard Baxter, *The Reformed Pastor* (London: James Nisbet and Co., 1860).

21. *Ibid.*, p. 128.

22. *Ibid.*, p. 130.

23. *Ibid.*

24. *Ibid.*, p. 131.

25. *Ibid.*

26. *Ibid.*

27. *Ibid.*, pp. 131–132.

28. *Ibid.*, p. 133.

29. *Ibid.*

30. Packer, *A Quest for Godliness* = *Among God's Giants*, pp. 399–400.

31. Baxter, *The Reformed Pastor*, pp. 133–135.

32. Packer, *A Quest for Godliness* = *Among God's Giants*, pp. 53–54.

33. *Ibid.*, pp. 400–401. A modern application of the Baxter model is found in Wallace Benn, *The Baxter Model: Guidelines for Pastoring Today* (Hartford: Fellowship of Word and Spirit, 1993).

34. G. Kittel and G. Friedrich (eds.), *Theological Dictionary of the New Testament* (Eng. trans. Grand Rapids: Eerdmans, 1964–76), vol. 3, p. 703.

35. The words are *kēryssein, legein, lalein, apophthengesthai, homilein, diēgeisthai, ekdiēgeisthai, exēgeisthai, dialegesthai, diermēneuein, gnōrizein, angelein, apangelein, anangelein, diangelein, exangelein, katangelein, euangelizesthai, parrēsiazomai, martyrein, epimartyrein, diamartyrein, peithein, homologein, krazein, prophēteuein, didaskein, paradidōmi, nouthetein, ton logon orthotomein, parakalein, elenkein, epitiman.*

36. *E.g.* Klaas Runia, 'What is Preaching according to the New Testament?' *Tyndale Bulletin* 29 (1978), pp. 3–48; Klaas Runia, *The Sermon under Attack* (Exeter: Paternoster, 1983), John Stott, *The Preacher's Portrait* (London: Tyndale, 1967); Jerome Murphy-O'Connor, *Paul on Preaching* (London and New York: Sheed and Ward, 1964), pp. 47ff.

37. The apparent exception to this 'Old Testament and then application' model is found in Acts 17. Here Paul begins with Old Testament theology, though not its language.

38. Quoted by David Peterson, 'The Ministry of Encouragement', in P. T. O'Brien and D. G. Peterson (eds.), *God who is Rich in Mercy* (Homebush West: Lancer, 1986), p. 240.

39. Richard Longenecker, *Biblical Exegesis in the Apostolic Period* (Grand Rapids: Eerdmans, 1975), p. 175.

40. See Murphy-O'Connor, *Paul on Preaching*.

5

The preacher's Bible

In Part 1 we looked at the biblical foundation of preaching and the great doctrines found in the Bible: *God has spoken*, *It is written*, and *Preach the Word*. In chapter 4 we looked at preaching as a form of the ministry of the Word, and developed from the Bible an expectation about preaching, what shape it should take and what it should achieve.

In this chapter we shall look at the preacher's Bible. We shall examine eight key issues which bear upon the relationship between the Bible and preaching, in order to see the practical implications of the Bible's nature and how it affects the way we prepare our sermons and preach. We shall cover Scripture's content, effectiveness, nature, relevance, use and dual authorship; biblical theology; and whether preaching also is the Word of God.

The content of Scripture: teach the Bible, or preach the message?

The issue we raise here is the relationship between the content of Scripture and the content of preaching. A helpful place to begin is with one of the model sermons of the New Testament that we have already discussed – Peter's sermon on the day of Pentecost in Acts 2. We can observe how the content of Scripture is related to the content of preaching.

Peter begins with the issue raised by the visible and audible coming of the Spirit on the day of Pentecost and the resulting preaching of the wonders of God in many different tongues. Peter addresses the issue in terms of the fulfilment of Joel 2 in the last days (Acts 2:17). His quotation from Joel ends with the words, 'and everyone who calls on the name of the Lord will be saved' (Acts 2:21). Peter thus opens with a citation from the Old Testament which is intended to make sense of the experience of the people on the day of Pentecost. He then includes what we now regard as 'New Testament' material, that is, information about the coming of Jesus of Nazareth and his significance (Acts 2:22–24). Peter returns to the Old Testament, his collection of quotations from the Psalms indicating the significance of Jesus in God's work of salvation. He explains the meaning of the psalms in terms 'of the resurrection of the Messiah' (Acts 2:31). He further comments that 'This Jesus God raised up, and of that all of us are witnesses' (2:32). The sermon ends with Peter instructing his hearers about what they should do in response to God's work in Christ, and his encouragement to them to do it.

For our purposes here, we notice that Peter makes use of what we might call 'Old Testament' and 'New Testament' material. His use of the Old Testament includes the references to Joel and the Psalms, and the 'New Testament' material is the information he gives his hearers about Jesus of Nazareth, his life, death and resurrection. Of course the New Testament had not yet been written, but the information that Peter gives is that which is later found within the New Testament. For Luke, then, the Christian sermon consists of what we now call Old Testament and New Testament information, as well as an application to the hearers of Peter's own day.

Christian preaching should continue to make use of the Old and New Testaments because, as we saw in chapter 1, the Old and New Testaments contain God's cumulative and enduring revelation for the sake of those who will believe in every generation. If God has worked in history to save his people, then the Scriptures of the Old and New Testaments are the only access we have to it. Furthermore, the Scriptures provide God's own interpretation of his actions, and this interpretation gives us access to God's revelation in history. P. T. Forsyth puts it this way: 'The great reason why the preacher must return continually to the Bible is that the Bible is the greatest sermon in the world. *Above every other function the Bible is a sermon, a kerugma, a preachment. It is the preacher's book because it is the preaching book.*'[1]

We need to clarify the relationship between the content of Scripture and our preaching. We have already noticed that Luke uses a number of phrases to describe New Testament preaching. These include 'the whole message about this life' (Acts 5:20), 'the word of God' (6:7), 'the good news about the kingdom of God and the name of Jesus Christ' (8:12), 'the good news' (8:25), 'the good news about Jesus' (8:35), 'the word of God' (11:1; 13:5), 'the good news of God's grace' (20:24), 'the kingdom' (20:25), 'the whole purpose of God' (20:27), 'the kingdom of God and . . . the Lord Jesus Christ' (28:31). It is important to notice the relationship between Scripture and the content of the message. We do not find that Luke characterizes early Christian preaching as preaching and teaching the Bible. Rather, he describes it in terms of the content of the message: the good news of God, the word of the Lord, the gospel about Jesus, the gospel of the Lord, and so on. This is despite the fact that those engaged in these ministries do make use of their Bible (the Old Testament) for their teaching and preaching ministry.

John Goldingay points out that the New Testament is a *midrash* (commentary) on Christ rather than on the Old Testament Scriptures,[2] but that it nevertheless presupposes the expository study of Scripture which has shaped the overall cast of mind of Jesus and the New Testament writers.[3]

We need to define the connection between the content of Scripture and preaching very carefully. For Luke the first Christian preachers made use of Scripture in order to teach or preach the good news of God, or the gospel of Christ, or the kingdom. That is to say, Scripture was a means to an end. I believe this is so for Christian preaching today. We must be absolutely committed to teaching and preaching the Bible, but to describe our ministry as 'teaching and preaching the Bible' is to describe it in terms of its means, not its end. The purpose of our teaching and preaching the Bible is to explain and commend the good news of God, the gospel of God, the gospel of God's grace, the kingdom of God and the Lord Jesus Christ.

This distinction between means and end, Scripture and message, has important implications for our prayers about our preaching, and for our expectation of our preaching and teaching ministry. If our sole aim is to preach and teach the Bible, to explain the Bible, to make clear the Bible, then we are serving only the means and not the ends, and our prayers will be limited as our vision is limited. Rather than 'Lord God, help me to teach the Bible today', our prayer ought to be, 'Lord God, help me to teach the Bible today so that people may understand and receive Jesus Christ and him crucified.' The distinction between means and ends has important implications for the content and style of our presentation. I am not saying that we should preach and teach Christ rather than preaching and teaching the Bible, but that we teach the Bible with the purpose of preaching Christ, or alternatively, we teach and preach Christ by means of teaching and preaching the Bible. Our teaching and preaching of Christ, then, are inextricably linked with communicating the content of the Bible; but the content of Scripture provides a means to an end, that is, preaching and teaching Christ.

The effectiveness of Scripture: it is useful

While current theological debate about Scripture concentrates on its authority, inspiration, infallibility and inerrancy, the New Testament has a different theological agenda. Its most important claim about Scripture (in this case the Old Testament) is that it is effective.

For example, Paul writes: 'Whatever was written in former days was written for our instruction, so that by steadfastness and by the encouragement of the scriptures we might have hope' (Rom. 15:4). Paul's assumption is that the Scriptures of the Old Testament were written to teach us (Christian believers), and that the result of their encouragement is that we might have hope. He assumes that the Scriptures work because they are the gift of God for Christian believers. The same point is made in the extended passage in which Paul encourages Timothy to see the value in ministry of the Word:

> But as for you, continue in what you have learned and firmly believed, knowing from whom you learned it, and how from childhood you have known the sacred writings that are able to instruct you for salvation through faith in Christ Jesus. All scripture is inspired by God and is useful for teaching, for reproof, for correction, and for training in righteousness. (2 Tim. 3:14–16)

Paul talks here about two ways in which the Scriptures are effective. First they 'are able to instruct you for salvation through faith in Christ Jesus'; that is, the Scriptures have the God-given power to make people understand what salvation is through faith in Christ Jesus. When Paul says that the Scriptures have this power he is, of course, using theological shorthand; he means that God gives the Scriptures this power, or that God uses Scripture for this purpose. Nevertheless, it remains true that for Paul Scripture itself is empowered by God to bring people to salvation in Christ Jesus. Secondly, Paul's point is that Scripture is both 'inspired by God' and also 'useful', and he describes this usefulness in terms of teaching, reproof, correcting, and training in righteousness. It is not clear whether Paul intends to say that Scripture teaches, reproves, corrects and trains in righteousness 'everyone who belongs to God' so that they may be 'equipped for every good work', or whether the primary reference is that Scripture is useful for Christian ministers in their ministry of teaching, reproving, correcting and training in righteousness. Perhaps both are true. The fact remains that Paul has this high expectation of the effectiveness of Scripture. It is in this context that he gives his famous encouragement in 4:2: 'Proclaim the message; be persistent whether the time is favourable or unfavourable; convince, rebuke and encourage, with the utmost patience in teaching.' This encouragement to Christian ministry is based on Paul's explanation of the function and effectiveness of Scripture. It is the Scriptures which provide the basis for Timothy's ministry of proclaiming the message, convincing, rebuking and encouraging with utmost patience in teaching.[4]

Peter has a similar view of the effectiveness of Scripture:

> You have been born anew, not of perishable but of imperishable seed, through the living and enduring Word of God. For,
> 'All flesh is like grass

and all its glory like the flower of grass.
The grass withers,
and the flower falls
but the Word of the Lord endures for ever.'
The word is the good news that was announced to you.
(1 Pet. 1:23–25)

We have already seen that Peter addresses those Christians who have been born again by the word preached to them, which is the living and enduring word of God, an imperishable seed, a word of the Lord which stands for ever.

This belief in the effectiveness of Scripture is of course a foundation stone of preaching. If we believed that Scripture was true but powerless, we would regard Christian preachers as those who have themselves the great responsibility of making the truth of God effective in people's lives. On the contrary, the assumption in the New Testament is that Scripture itself is effective, and our hope for our ministry of preaching and teaching the Bible must be based on this assumption, confidence and hope. We are preaching not a dead word but a living Word: we are preaching not a word which is ineffective but a Word which is effective in the hand of God, for God's own good purposes. We can thus preach with confidence, faith and expectation.

The nature of Scripture: propositions or poetry?

What then is our view of the nature of Scripture of which we make use in our preaching?

R. E. C. Browne, in his book *The Ministry of the Word*,[5] contrasts two models of revelation and relates them to two styles of preaching. He claims that a view of Scripture as propositional revelation results in preaching which is largely propositional.[6] That is to say, a belief that the Bible contains truths about God, and about the kind of lives that Christians are called to lead, will result in a kind of preaching which conveys truths about God and about how we ought to live in response to God's revelation. Browne contrasts this with a more poetic view of revelation in which the Bible writers are free agents and are able to use their imaginations to try and understand what God has done. He suggests that this view of the Bible will result in preaching which also enables preachers to exercise more freedom, creativity and imagination.

David Buttrick also comments on this direct relationship between the preacher's view of Scripture and the preacher's view of preaching.

Thus, for example, if Scripture is viewed as an inerrant Word of God, sermons are apt to come tumbling down from high

91

pulpits like tablets of stone from Sinai. If, in a Barthian scheme, Scripture is understood as a God-ordained witness to the Word of God, Jesus Christ, then preaching is regarded as a witness to the witness of Scripture, and a reiteration of the Word of God. On the other hand, if preaching is vested in an episcopate within the being-saved community, preaching will be defined as an extension of the preaching of bishops. In Pietist communities, preaching may be viewed as an expression of the awareness of being saved undergirded by the authority of primal religious experience.[7]

There is often a direct link between a theology of Scripture and a theology of preaching because both depend on a prior theology of revelation. In terms of the issue as defined by Browne, if revelation is seen as propositional, Scripture will be viewed as propositional and so will preaching; if revelation is regarded as poetic, Scripture will be understood as poetry and a poetic style of preaching will be followed.

The contrast between the propositional and poetic views of Scripture and preaching put forward by Browne is highly problematic. It depends on a definition of propositional revelation and of poetic revelation which treats them as mutually exclusive. We could look, however, at the first three verses of Psalm 1:

> Happy are those
>   who do not follow the advice of the wicked,
> or take the path that sinners tread,
>   or sit in the seat of scoffers;
> but their delight is in the law of the LORD,
>   and on his law they meditate day and night.
> They are like trees
>   planted by streams of water,
> which yield their fruit in its season,
>   and their leaves do not wither.
> In all that they do, they prosper.

This is obviously in poetic form and yet it makes statements which can only be regarded as propositional. Perhaps Browne's distinction between poetry and proposition is an unhelpful one.

In general terms, the debate about propositional and poetic revelation over the past hundred years has taken the following form. First, the idea of propositional, doctrinal and objective revelation has traditionally been supported by Roman Catholic and Protestant orthodoxy. Secondly, writers influenced by the Enlightenment, the Romantic movement, existentialism, the 'God who acts' movement, neo-orthodoxy and liberalism have rejected the idea of propositional revelation and suggested different models of revelation to replace it. Thirdly, in response to this wholesale rejection, conservative evangelical scholars have supported and defended propositional revelation as being the key to revelation. This has affected their understanding not only of the Bible but also of preaching.

Among modern evangelical scholars, Paul Helm defends a positive view of propositional revelation against its critics, and gives its biblical and theological context. According to Helm, those who oppose propositional revelation criticize it for being concerned with timeless ahistorical truths, for being basically philosophical in style, for not demanding a personal response, and for being an alternative to revelation of a person.[8] Helm demonstrates that biblical propositional revelation is in fact historical rather than timeless, that it is not a matter of philosophical statement but of revealed truth, that propositional revelation always demands a personal response, and that it is unhelpful to see propositions as 'merely words'. 'There is no antithesis between believing a proposition and believing a person if the proposition is understood as the assertion of the person.'[9]

Leon Morris also joins the debate between the opponents and proponents of propositional revelation. He says that Christianity 'is basically a gospel "good news". And "good news" has content.'[10] He goes on to say:

> To hold to propositional revelation is not to insist that the Bible is a series of infallible propositions laid side by side for our inspection and assimilation. Some of the Bible may well be held to come under this description, as for example the proposition God is love (1 Jn. 4:8). But much of the Bible is not susceptible of this kind of treatment. Often the exegete must wrestle with difficult problems if he is to come up with the meaning of the text. Most of us would agree that no superficial study can do justice to say, the book of Job or the Epistle to the Romans . . . But it is to insist that, when due regard is to be had to all the proper procedures of the exegete, what he comes up with has conceptual content. It is capable of being given expression.[11]

J. I. Packer puts it well when he says:

> Not that the text of Scripture is made up entirely of formal doctrinal statements; of course, it is not . . . comparatively little of Scripture consists of systematic theological exposition; most of it is of a different order. Broadly speaking, the Bible is an interpretative record of sacred history. It reports God's words to Israel, and His dealings with them, down the ages. It includes biographies, meditations, prayers and praises which show us

how faith and unbelief, obedience and disobedience, temptation and conflict, work out in practice in human lives. It contains much imaginative matter – poetical, rhetorical, parabolic, visionary – which sets before our minds in a vivid, concrete and suggestive way great general principles, the formal statement of which has often to be sought in other contexts. In fact, Scripture is an organism, a complex, self-interpreting whole, its theology showing the meaning of the events and experiences which it records, and the events and experiences show the outworking of the theology in actual life. All these items have their place in the total system of biblical truth.[12]

This diversity of biblical material can be clearly demonstrated from the book of Revelation. Revelation contains statements that could be described as propositional in style: for example, 'Holy, holy, holy, the Lord God the Almighty, who was and is and is to come' (4:8) and 'Worthy is the Lamb that was slaughtered to receive power and wealth and wisdom and might and honour and glory and blessing!' (5:12). It would be perfectly possible to take other verses of Revelation and turn them into propositional statements, and to provide a summary of the book in terms of propositions. We could begin as follows: The book of Revelation is the revelation of Jesus Christ which God gave Jesus to show to his servants. He made it known by sending his angel to his servant John who testified to everything that he saw. There is a blessing on the one who reads aloud the words of the prophecy, and on those who hear and keep what is written in it. God sends grace and peace to the seven churches in the province of Asia (1:1–4), and so on.

This might be a helpful exercise in summarizing the teaching of the book of Revelation. Perhaps it would be a useful way in for a young Christian who does not know the book. But the book of Revelation is more than a series of propositions, so to claim that its message can be adequately conveyed by propositions derived from it is surely not true. For the impact of the book lies not only in the truths it conveys but also in the images it uses in order to convey those truths and in its apocalyptic language and imagery. To put the issue another way, if the Bible is 'the greatest sermon in the world',[13] we have to recognize that the form of God's sermon is not a series of propositions but a great variety of styles of communication, including propositions, parables, history, sayings, apocalyptic, warnings and narrative. If this is the style of Scripture, perhaps it ought also to be the style of our preaching.

My argument for the value of propositional revelation contradicts many contemporary assumptions. Gabriel Hebert says:

Throughout Scripture the Word of God is conveyed often by means other than those of plain historical statement; by poetry

> and by tales . . . through the symbolism of the sacrifices, and in the sacraments of the New Covenant. All these in their various ways speak the Word of God on a deeper level than that of logically reasoned argument or historical narrative.[14]

Hebert's claim that poetry, tales, symbolism and sacraments speak the word of God on a 'deeper level' than that of logically reasoned argument or historical narrative is very misleading. In the first place, as we have seen, the Bible's logically reasoned arguments and historical narrative convey the truth-claims of the personal God. Secondly, Hebert does not make it clear in what ways poetry, tales, symbolism and sacraments speak on a 'deeper level'. Is the imagery of a deeper level meant to reflect theological or psychological truth? In what ways do stories operate at a deeper level? Hebert's claim is a common assumption of modern-day practical anthropology and of Christian theologians, but, as we have already claimed, words and content-full statements are at the heart of our very deepest relationships. Relationships function by means other than words, as well as by words, but Hebert's claim that propositions do not function at a deep level is unsupported.

So far we have described the debate as conducted between conservative evangelicals (who are in favour of propositional revelation) and other theologians (who are opposed to propositional revelation and in favour of poetic revelation or some other form). It is worth noting a comment of James Barr:

> What has been expressed as an issue about propositional revelation seems mostly to have been not an issue about propositions (as against non-propositional communication) but one about the recognition of the *right function* of propositions . . . the issue here is a literary category mistake, not a question whether the material is propositional or not.[15]

As Barr points out, one of the questions that relates to our subject is a right understanding of the different literary genres of the Bible.

Donald Bloesch issues a warning against modern evangelical preoccupation with propositional revelation.

> The bane of much of modern evangelicalism is rationalism which presupposes that the Word of God is directly available to human reason. It is fashionable to refer to the biblical revelation as propositional, and in one sense this is true in that the divine revelation is communicated through verbal concepts and models. It signifies that revelation has a noetic as well as a personal dimension, that it is conceptual as well as experiential.

Revelation includes both the events of divine self-disclosure and biblical history and their prophetic and apostolic inter-pretation. At the same time we must not infer that the propositional statements in the Bible are themselves revealed, since this makes the Bible the same kind of book as the Koran which purports to be exclusively divine. It also seems to imply a transubstantiation of the human word into the divine word. The Bible is not directly the revelation of God but indirectly in that God's Word comes to us through the mode of human instrumentality. Revelation is better spoken of as polydimen-sional rather than propositional in the strict sense, in that it connotes the event of God's speaking as well as the truth of what is spoken: the truth, moreover, takes various linguistic forms including the propositional.[16]

Bloesch makes a number of points here which are worth evaluating. First, he is right to say that propositional revelation signifies that revelation has a noetic and conceptual dimension. This is the very point that evangelicals have been trying to preserve in the current debate. Secondly, Bloesch wants to avoid the idea that the propositional statements in the Bible are themselves revealed, though he will allow the status of revelation to the prophetic and apostolic interpretation of divine events. It is not clear how Bloesch can separate prophetic and apostolic interpretation, which is revelation, from the statements in the Bible, for in many cases the prophets and apostles are the authors of those statements. Bloesch's accusation that to believe that propositional statements are revealed is to make the Bible the same kind of book as the Koran is misleading. Biblical scholars do not claim that the Bible is exclusively divine or a transubstantiation of the human word in the divine word. They do believe that the Bible is directly the revelation of God, as well as the product of human authors. Thirdly, Bloesch's suggestion that revelation should be spoken of as poly-dimensional is helpful if one of those dimensions is propositional revelation. The other dimensions include the personal presence of God, the acts of God and the various other linguistic forms in which God speaks. Fourthly, we need to assert against Bloesch that the Bible is directly the revelation of God. God's Spirit does illuminate the mind of the readers to see the meaning of the words of Scripture, but he also caused those words to be written. Personal illumination is no substitute for verbal inspiration; the words *are* the revelation, not just a witness to the revelation; the Bible's words are not 'one step removed'[17] from revelation, they *are* the revelation.

The point of this discussion has been to seek a way forward in the current debate between propositionalists and non-propositionalists. I have tried to show that any view of revelation which is true to the Bible must contain the idea that the Bible includes propositions, but also that it cannot be claimed that revelation is given exclusively in terms of propositions. If this is true of revelation, it is true of the Bible (in which we find propositions about God and what he requires of human beings), and also of many other forms of revelation. If this is true of the Bible, it will also necessarily be true of our preaching, which should exhibit the same variety and pluriformity. If the Bible is *God* preaching, then *our* preaching should echo and resonate with his preaching.

The consequence of this is that if our preaching contains no intellectual, conceptual or propositional content, it is not true to the Bible. Conversely, if all our preaching does is convey intellectual, conceptual content, we may equally well claim that it is not being true to the Bible. Our preaching should convey, not reduce, the intellectual and emotional impact of our text.

The relevance of Scripture: bridging the gap

The crucial issue for the preacher is the relevance of Scripture. If the fundamental understanding of ourselves and of our congregation is that Scripture is irrelevant, we shall have to work very hard if we want to bridge the gap. Conversely, if our assumption and that of our hearers is that Scripture is relevant to our lives then we will not have to do so much spade-work in demonstrating the relevance of any part of Scripture, let alone the whole of Scripture.

The arguments for the relevance of Scripture lie within the structure of chapter 1. These include the theological assumption that God's spoken and written revelation is cumulative, that God speaks with a future audience in mind, that the Old Testament Scriptures are preserved for Christian use, and that the historical revelation in Christ is of significance for all people throughout the world for all time. Thus the relevance of Scripture is ultimately tied to the relevance of Christ, and the decisive and normative revelation in Scripture reflects the fact that 'in these last days [God] has spoken to us by a Son' (Heb. 1:2). The revelation in Christ and the revelation in Scripture are tied together. As James Smart puts it, without the Bible 'the remembered Christ becomes the imagined Christ, shaped by the religiosity and the unconscious desires of his worshippers'.[18]

Against our assertion of the relevance of Scripture, many voices in our age assume the irrelevance or obsolescence of Scripture. We should not be surprised at this, for Scripture represents both an authority which is objective and external for people who read it or hear about it, and a voice which speaks from the past.

The first objection is that Scripture comes from outside the thought-world and experience of those who read or hear it. All the great movements of western intellectual and cultural life over the past three centuries have resulted in an opposition to Scripture as an external authority. One effect of the Enlightenment was that people distrusted any external or objective authority, and the individual became the one who had the responsibility of assessing and understanding what was true and significant. The Romantic movement was similarly self-centred. Here the question was not so much conformity to the rational assumptions or conclusions of individuals, but a sense of resonance with deeper personal and cosmic reality. But the test still remained with the individual. In our own time existentialism has had a powerful effect, and has again assumed that the primary responsibility to determine and to define the nature of reality lies with the individual. The evident self-centred nature of these movements has resulted in a society reluctant to attribute authority or significance beyond the bounds of its own reason, experience or imagination. Any religion which claims an objective reality will find it hard to make headway in this context.

The Christian faith depends not only on an external authority and source of revelation but also on one which is rooted in history. It is not surprising to find considerable opposition to the idea of historical faith emerging in our lifetime. This has been expressed most conveniently in Dennis Nineham's *The Use and Abuse of the Bible*.[19] Nineham provides a useful example. As a liberal scholar he is expressing in theological language the common thoughts of the average person in the street. The great benefit of studying liberal theologians is that we can thereby attune ourselves to what ordinary people think. I suspect we will find this thinking not only in the street but also within our churches, particularly as people come into our churches who do not have a strong foundation of Christian teaching or share the assumptions of Christian values or priorities.

Nineham's argument is one of cultural relativism. The problem is not understanding what an ancient document *meant*, but understanding what it *means*. Nineham believes that though we are able to grasp what biblical writers meant, we cannot believe what they believed. Our beliefs about natural science, historical enquiry and so on, render what the Bible says frankly incredible.[20] As Paul Helm points out, Nineham's belief is not that the Bible writers are wrong and we are right, or that they are more wrong than we, but that neither they nor we are correct.[21] 'Each of us, our ancestors, ourselves and our successors are culturally bound, our thinking is dominated by different mind-sets, sets of presuppositions and assumptions.'[22]

Nineham pushes his argument too far to be conclusive. If we believe in an absolute cultural relativism, it is impossible for us to know what first-century writers meant. Our problem is not that we do not know what they meant, but that we do know what they meant and we find it hard to believe. Perhaps the point of Nineham's argument is that it does reflect a view common in our community, whether it is Henry Ford's 'History is bunk' or the average person's assumption that anything that happened in the past is unknowable or irrelevant. Those of us who are preachers have to deal with this in commending the Christian gospel.

The gap between the Bible writers and ourselves can easily be overstated or misrepresented. For example, a large part of our work on 1 Corinthians must be to try to work out what had happened at Corinth, what the Corinthians believed, what was the content of the letter they wrote to Paul, and what was the content of other messages Paul had received, and thus to understand Paul's writing of 1 Corinthians in that context of thought. This is no small task, but if a copy of 1 Corinthians came to first-century Rome or Ephesus the good Christians there would have had the same problems that we have. They may have had more immediate means of finding the answers to their questions, but nevertheless the basic problem remains; they would have needed to find some way of understanding the situation in Corinth to which 1 Corinthians responds. Although we see ourselves as people of the late twentieth century, for whom the past is out of date and irrelevant, another aspect of our society is an intense desire to return to the past, to uncover its wisdom and to learn from it. A society which is now talking about Gaia can scarcely claim that it views the past as irrelevant.

The basis of the relevance of Scripture is that Scripture addresses two audiences: that is, the revelation has a dual purpose. It is the 'then and now' of Scripture which provides the key. For Scripture was originally addressed to those who lived two or three thousand years ago. It was addressed to them in their language, in thought forms which they could understand, and largely by their contemporaries. It was God's purpose that the first readers of Deuteronomy, Exodus, Proverbs, Jeremiah, Mark, Ephesians and Revelation would understand these words as God's address to them. But, as we have seen, Scripture is also intended to address later readers as well, including ourselves. Scripture is not only the record of God's words of revelation in times past, it is also God speaking to us now. We represent the (chronologically) second audience of Scripture. God had both audiences in mind. The implication of this dual purpose of Scripture in addressing God's people then and God's people now is that we must not short-circuit the process of explaining the meaning of Scripture.

If a liberal view is that Scripture is primarily addressed to people in the past but that we may listen in if we will, then a common 'fundamentalist' view is that Scripture is God speaking to us now without reference to God's address to the first audience, that is, his people two or three thousand years ago. To view Scripture as God speaking to us now without referring to the first audience is to turn Scripture into a supra-historical document and to remove it from its historical context and meaning.

Our movement of interpretation must always be to ask, 'What did it mean then?' and go on to ask, 'What does it mean now?' Scripture is God's Word *then* which he preserved for us *now*, and this dual purpose of the revelation is an integral part of the significance and effective use of Scripture.[23]

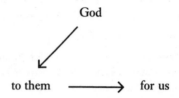

If we keep this dual purpose of the revelation in mind we shall avoid the trap of reading Scripture as if it were a twentieth-century document. Reading Scripture as if it were a twentieth-century document is dangerous, since we would automatically read it with twentieth-century meanings in our minds and miss the original intention of God through the human authors of Scripture. Without this awareness of the gap between our own age and the first century, we may miss the fact that a difference in horizon may mean a difference in meaning. Anthony Thiselton writes of the 'negative possibility of transforming meaning unwittingly by failing to note the differences and distinctiveness which characterise the horizons of the biblical text in contrast to our own'.[24]

Can we recover the original form of the revelation? Can a revelation given in former times be relevant to our age? How do we allow for the great intellectual, moral and cultural distance which stands between ourselves and the Bible writers? Do we treat ancient documents with integrity if we remove them from their original context? Do we do so if we attempt to give them a contemporary relevance? It is worth noting that these questions relating to our use of Scripture are only one aspect of the problems raised by any form of historical revelation. At heart the issue is not the contemporaneity of Christ's words, but the contemporary significance of Christ. In my opinion, the fundamental issue of revelation in history must be tackled first, and then the contemporary relevance of Scripture as the living God continuing to speak falls into place.

John Macquarrie makes the positive point that Christianity contains a classic or primordial revelation.

> A community of faith, within which a theology arises, usually traces its history back to what may be called a 'classic' or 'primordial' revelation. This classic revelation, a definite disclosive experience of the holy granted to the founder or founders of the community, becomes as it were the paradigm

> for experiences of the holy in that community. A revelation that
> has the power to found a community of faith becomes fruitful
> in that community, and is, so to speak, repeated or re-enacted in
> the experience of the community, thus becoming normative for
> the experience of the community. Yet only because the
> primordial revelation is continually renewed in present
> experience can it be revelation for us, and not just a fossilised
> revelation.[25]

What Macquarrie refers to as the 'renewal' of the primordial revelation
he elsewhere describes as its repetition, by which he means 'going into
some experience that has been handed down in such a way that it is, so to
speak, brought into the present and its insights and possibilities made alive
again'.[26] It seems to me that Macquarrie falls into the trap of assuming that
this process of 'repetition' is only a human process. It is of course a divine
action of revelation, in which the primordial revelation is reapplied to the
believer by the power of the self-revealing God.

Most of the questions rehearsed above make the mistake of assuming
that the biblical revelation was intended by God only for those of long
ago, and that it is our task to 'apply it', or 'make it relevant' to a later age.
But my argument is that God's intention was that the historic revelation
would serve future generations.[27] Working out how it does so is not
always easy; but I believe that we ought to tackle the difficulties with the
assumption that Scripture is God's Word for today, and not assume that
it is not.[28]

The problem of ' the pastness of the past' is often put to the preacher in
terms of the 'two horizons', one of the original author, and the other of
the modern reader.[29] I think the problem can be overstated, with
paralysing results. I try to work on the problem with the following
correctives in mind. First, I assume that my common humanity with the
Bible writers will result in some instinctive resonance of understanding.
Second, I recognize that a 'horizon' is of course subjectively determined,
and try to reduce the limitations of my horizon by study and imagination,
and by my understanding of their horizon as well. Third, I believe that in
some cases at least, the human authors of Scripture had a future audience
in mind (see, e.g., 1 Pet. 1:10–11). Fourth, I recognize that to speak of
human authors is to give only half the picture. If God is in some sense the
author of Scripture, was his horizon limited? Fifth, I believe that God had
a future audience in mind when he caused Scripture to be written – or
better, we are the same audience, the one people of God, the one
household and temple of God, made up of Jews and Gentiles, fellow heirs
of God's promises to Israel, members of one body, and sharers together in
the promise in Christ Jesus (Eph. 2:19 – 3:6). Sixth, although we
emphasize the real gap between ourselves and the first century AD, from

God's point of view we live in the same age, the 'last days' between the first and second comings of Christ. Seventh, God, the author, is still alive, and can still use his words by his Spirit. Eighth, I am not an individual reader, but part of a community of faith – and together we hear the words of God. Finally, words and ideas can be culturally expressed without being culturally limited.

The use of Scripture: getting it right

If all we had to do was to read out Scripture believing that it was the Word of God, and if the public reading of the Scripture were sufficient, then the task of the minister of the Word would be a lot easier. But our task is to select a portion of Scripture and preach and teach it to our congregation. Even if we are fully convinced of the trustworthiness, sufficiency, authority and relevance of Scripture, there still remains the difficult task of teaching it in a responsible way and applying it to the lives of the people before us.

We can recognize the difficulty easily enough by pointing to common ways in which Scripture is misused. Here are some examples.

A verse of Scripture may be taken out of context and so misunderstood. An early prooftext that I remember learning as a young Christian was Habbakuk 1:13, 'Your eyes are too pure to behold evil.' The point was assumed to be the moral purity and incorruptibility of God, before whose presence sinners could not stand. I remember my great shock and delight when I studied Habakkuk for the first time and discovered that the words form part of Habakkuk's complaint against God that God was planning to use evil people for his purposes. The meaning I learnt as a young Christian was theologically true, though this particular text was used inaccurately to support it.

The text may be used as a launching-pad for a discussion of some other subject as a mere issue-raiser. The commonly quoted warning against this is that 'a text without a context is a pretext'. One minister with whom I worked saw every sermon as an excuse to preach on the centrality of the Bible in home and national life. No matter what text he began with, this was the substance of his sermon. While the theme he fixed on was a good one, it was perhaps inappropriate to preach it as the meaning and application of every text he could find.

Another misuse of the text is to 'psychologize' Scripture. Any human issue or psychological state referred to in the text then becomes a peg for the preacher's latest theories on these subjects. At a more sophisticated level, the preacher may appear to be preaching on a passage of Scripture while in fact preaching on a psychological subtext which he or she has read into the passage.

A further example is that of moralizing from the text. I remember a resolute sermon on Philippians 3:13, 'this one thing I do', which took as its theme the importance of having aims in life. Unfortunately, none of the aims suggested by the preacher approximated to the aim enunciated by Paul, who continued: 'Forgetting what is behind and straining forward to what lies ahead, I press on towards the goal for the prize of the heavenly call of God in Christ Jesus' (3:13–14).

Another example of inappropriate use of Scripture is to 'doctrinalize' Scripture. In this case Scripture becomes no more than a set of prooftexts to support the particular doctrinal preferences of the preacher. This usually results in a range of about twenty doctrinal sermons being preached, with the content the same on every occasion, though the entry point will differ according to the text being used at the time.

My final example is that of preaching on the gaps between the words. 'Now the Bible doesn't tell us how Mary felt about this. But I am sure that she felt . . . and so we ought to . . .'

What then can we say about the honest and positive use of the Bible for the preacher? Sidney Greidanus suggests the following considerations for properly bridging the gap. *Concentrate on the original message.* Ask: what issues did the author seek to address? What questions did he seek to answer? What is the specific message he proclaimed? *Recognize the discontinuity.* We need to recognize the gap between the original audience of the message and ourselves. *Recognize the overarching continuity.* Greidanus identifies this as the constancy of God's character and purpose and the continuity of God's people. Finally, *focus on the goal of the text.*[30]

With these purposes in mind, what is the aim of the sermon with regard to Scripture? I would suggest the following.

We should teach the content of Scripture. Many of the people before us will be ignorant of the content of the Bible, and we should not assume knowledge which is not present. Time taken to explain the content of the passage we are preaching from is time well spent.

We should teach the purpose of Scripture. The content of the text is not neutral. We shall need to bring out its purposes and implications for those who are hearing. We must make sure that the content of our sermon derives in every part from Scripture, that is, that the basis, content and application conform to the purpose for which Scripture was originally given.

We should model a good use of Scripture. One of the most useful things we can do for our hearers is to model a good hermeneutic – that is, an accurate understanding of the text in its immediate context and in the context of the whole Bible, followed by relevant application to people's lives. This modelling process is helpful whether we begin with a text and apply it to people's lives, or whether we adopt the other method, raising an issue of everyday life and then heading towards Scripture to find a suitable and godly response to it. Either way we should be modelling an appropriate use of Scripture to our hearers. As Augustine said:

He who reads to an audience pronounces aloud the words he sees before him, he who teaches reading does it that others may be able to read for themselves. Each, however, communicates to others what he has learnt himself. Just so, the man who explains to an audience the passage of Scripture he understands is like one who reads aloud the words before. On the other hand, the man who lays down rules for interpretation is like the one who teaches reading, that is, shows others how to read for themselves.[31]

We should aim to encourage people to test what we say by Scripture. Our stance is not that we are masters of Scripture and people are subject to our interpretation. Rather, together, preachers and hearers alike are under Scripture and so the words of the preacher can be judged by the congregation according to how far they conform to God's will as revealed in Scripture.[32]

The dual authorship of Scripture: divine and human writers

Scripture has a dual authorship. God is the author of every part of Scripture through his Spirit, yet at the same time he did not exercise his authorship without involving human authors at every point. J. I. Packer describes this dual authorship in these terms:

[God] was well able to prepare, equip and overrule sinful human writers so that they wrote nothing but what he intended; and the Scripture tells us that this is what in fact he did. We are to think of the Spirit's inspiring activity, and for that matter, of all his regular operations in and upon personality as (to use an old and valuable technical term) *concursive*; that is, as exercised in, through and by means of the writers' own activity, in such a way that their thinking and writing was *both* free and spontaneous on their part *and* divinely elicited and controlled, and what they wrote was not only their work but also God's work.[33]

Packer suggests that a helpful model for understanding this dual authorship is the way in which God regularly works through human beings to achieve his will. In the same way we can see Scripture as a result both of the intervention of God and of the human authors' activities and intentions.

We can observe this dual authorship in the way in which the author of the letter to the Hebrews refers to the Old Testament in his quotations of

Psalm 95 in chapters 3 and 4. He introduces the quotations in three ways. In Hebrews 3:7 he says, 'Therefore, as the Holy Spirit says', clearly identifying the author of Psalm 95 as the Holy Spirit. In 4:3 he writes 'just as God has said' before introducing his next quotation from Psalm 95, again identifying the author as God. A few verses later in 4:7 he introduces the quotation with these words: '[God] sets a certain day – "today" – saying through David much later, in the words already quoted, "Today, if you hear his voice, do not harden your hearts."' As far as the writer of the letter to the Hebrews is concerned, God the Holy Spirit is the author of Psalm 95, but he spoke these words through King David.

J. I. Packer suggests three different psychological forms of inspiration. He describes the basic form as that of *dualistic inspiration*, 'in which the recipient of revelation remained conscious throughout of the distinction between himself, the hearer and reporter, and God, the Speaker to and through him'.[34] This inspiration, Packer says, produced prophetic oracles and apocalyptic visions. He also describes what he calls *lyric inspiration*, in which 'the inspiring action of God was fused with the concentrating, intensifying and shaping mental processes of what, in a secular sense, we would call the inspiration of the poet'.[35] This produced the Psalms, the lyric, the drama of Job, the Song of Solomon, and the great prayers. His other example is *organic inspiration*, 'whereby the inspiring action of God coalesces with the mental processes – inquiring, analytical, reflective, interpretive, applicatory – of the teacher, seeking to distil and pass on knowledge of facts and right thoughts about them. This type of inspiration produced the historical books of both Testaments, the apostolic letters, and, in the Old Testament, the books of Proverbs and Ecclesiastes.'[36] I am not certain if I would agree with Packer's three categories, but at least we ought to recognize that the divine super-intendence of human authorship may have been experienced in different ways by different people at different times.

What does it mean to respect the divine authorship of Scripture? It means to recognize the authority of Scripture as being the authority of God himself in his words. For God's words represent his will, his plan, his promise, his warning and his encouragement, and as we respond to God's words we respond to God himself. It also means to respect the coherence and unity of Scripture. Although we can recognize God's working through human authors at different times and in different places, so that Scripture often speaks with a varied voice, nevertheless we should be looking for the coherence and unity that are produced by the mind of the primary author, God. Because the Bible is God's words, we should also expect to find that the words of God are useful and have contemporary power to bring salvation to us, to change us, and to transform us.

At the same time, if we are to be true to the nature of Scripture as we understand it, we must also respect the human authors whom God chose and used for his purposes. This means respecting the diversity of Scripture, and the intention of the secondary authors in their writing as being an element in our understanding of what they say. It also means that we must pay attention to the historical and theological context in which the authors wrote, their place in salvation history and the way in which their work would have been read by God's people at the time of writing. It means too that we should cope with a variety of literary styles and different use of language, so that we recognize, for example, that the one word 'faith' may be used in a variety of ways by different New Testament writers, or that dense theological argument is not the same as parable, narrative, or prophecy. We misread, misunderstand and misuse Scripture if we do not take account of both its divine and its human authorship. In a later section of this chapter we will examine further these ways of respecting the divine and human authors of Scripture in our study of the theology of Scripture. But before doing so we must consider whether or not the incarnation of Christ, his divine and human natures, provides a helpful analogy to the divinity and humanity of Scripture.

The divinity and humanity of Scripture is an aspect of the issue we have been discussing, the dual authorship of Scripture. The question is the relationship between the doctrines of inscripturation and incarnation. Is there an analogy between the two? If Christ is the Word become flesh, is the Bible the Word become Scripture? 'Since the divine and human factors come into play with Christ as well as with Scripture, could not the God-breathed character of Scripture be illuminated in a significant way by the incarnation and its 'union of two natures?'[37] Berkouwer discusses this issue in his chapter entitled 'The Servant Form of Holy Scripture'. He refers to Bavinck's statement about Scripture as 'the incarnation of the Word',[38] and to his assertion that incarnation and inscripturation are not only analogous 'but are also very intimately related'.[39] A similar view is expressed in Pius XII's *Divino afflante Spiritu*: 'Just as the substantial Word of God became like to men in all things, sin excepted . . . so the words of God, expressed in human language, became in all things like to human speech, error excepted.'[40]

How should we respond to this idea?

First, the analogy between Christ and the Bible appears closer than it is because of the use of 'word' in the phrases 'the incarnation of the Word' and 'the inscripturation of the words'. The common use of 'word' is powerful, but deceptive. To avoid this linguistic lure, it is more helpful to pose the question in slightly different terms, speaking of the relation between 'the incarnation of the Son' and 'the inscripturation of God's speech'. This allows a more nuanced discussion to take place.

Secondly, if there is any analogy between the incarnation of the Son and the inscripturation of God's speech it is certainly subject to severe limitations. Warfield states: 'There is no hypostatic union between the divine and human in Scripture, we cannot parallel the "inscripturation" of the Holy Spirit and the incarnation of the Son of God.'[41] We may and must worship the Son of God, but we may not worship the Bible. And while God could in theory add to the Bible (another book of Proverbs?), it is impossible to think of 'adding' to the Son. J. I. Packer comments: 'At best, the analogy between the divine-human person of the Word made flesh, who is Christ, and the divine-human product of the Word written, which is Scripture, can only be a limited one.'[42]

Thirdly, as Packer notes, the debate about the divinity and humanity of Christ is similar to the debate about the divine and human authorship of the Bible. He quotes Gabriel Hebert and Reginald Fuller as attacking orthodox Christians as monophysite in Christology, denying the full humanity of Christ, and similarly denying the human authorship of the Scriptures. He quotes Fuller: 'All the way through, we have to discern the treasure in the earthen vessels: the divinity in Christ's humanity . . . the Word of God in the fallible words of men.'[43]

Packer replies by accusing the liberals of a Nestorian view of Christ:

> Nestorianism begins by postulating a distinction between Jesus as a man and the divine Son, whom it regards as someone distinct, indwelling the man; but then it cannot conceive of the real personal identity of the man and the Son. The right and scriptural way in Christology is to start by recognizing the unity of our Lord's Person as divine and to view His humanity only as an aspect of His Person, existing within it and never, therefore, dissociated from it. Similarly, the right way to think of Scripture is to start from the biblical idea that the written Scriptures as such are 'the oracles of God' and to study their character as a human book only as one aspect of their character as a divine book.[44]

The parallel between the doctrine of Christ and the doctrine of the Bible is most clearly seen in discussions about fallibility, error, sinfulness and cultural limitations. Liberal Christians assume that humanity necessarily involves fallibility, error, sinfulness and cultural limitations, and this affects their doctrine of both Christ and the Bible. Because orthodox Christians begin with the divine origin of both Christ and the Bible, they are less likely to attribute fallibility, error, sinfulness or cultural limitations to either. Just as in Christology we need an understanding that does justice to both the divinity and the humanity of Christ, so in our doctrine of Scripture we need to do justice to both the divine and the human authorship of the Bible.

Even if the analogy between Christ and Scripture is remote, it is nevertheless illuminating. As we have seen, doctrines of Christ and of the

Bible are often compatible, and spring from prior theological beliefs about the relationship between God and the world, the way God relates to human beings, and the essential feature of human activity.

Orthodox Christians should guard against undervaluing the humanity of Christ and the human authors of Scripture. Liberal Christians need to guard against undervaluing the divinity of Christ and the divine authorship of Scripture.

Finally, if the analogy of the divinity and humanity of Christ is at all helpful in understanding Scripture, it might be good to complement it with other models of divine and human activity. What we are trying to find is a comparable example in which there is an appropriate balance between divine initiative and sovereignty on the one hand and human activity on the other.

Paul describes the governing authorities as 'God's servant' (Rom. 13:4). While the governing authorities are not infallible, it is not impossible to imagine a situation where the punishment they inflict is, in God's eyes, appropriate to the crime. The punishment is then both God's action, and the action of the governing authorities – both a divine and a human action.

Elsewhere, Paul describes us as 'what [God] has made us, created in Christ Jesus for good works, which God prepared beforehand to be our way of life' (Eph. 2:10). Though we are sinners, we may still do 'good works', because we are saved by grace, and created in Christ Jesus to do the good works that God has prepared for us to do. Though I am a sinner, and everything I do is affected by my sinfulness, yet, in God's mercy, I may do a good work, and this good work is both God's and mine; its goodness comes from God, but its particular human shape and expression come from me. This is perhaps another analogy for Scripture, in which God's work and human expression are combined. For the humanity of Scripture is reflected most clearly in the great diversity of styles of vocabulary and literature that it contains.

D. M. Baillie's *God was in Christ* may prove illuminating at this point.[45] Baillie attempts to explain the incarnation by means of the 'paradox of grace'. Of this paradox Baillie says that 'its essence lies in the conviction which a Christian man possesses, that every good thing in him, every good thing he does, is somehow not wrought by himself, but God'.[46] And later he claims 'that this paradox in its fragmentary form in our own Christian lives is a reflection of that perfect union of God and man in the incarnation on which the whole Christian life depends, and may therefore be our best clue to the understanding of it'.[47] Baillie recognizes that 'on the one hand there is Jesus making His human choice from moment to moment . . . on the other hand, all His words and all His choices depended on the Father'.[48] The central paradox, 'Not I, but the grace of God' is the clue to understanding Christ as well as Christians.[49]

If those who see a close parallel between Christ and the Bible are in danger of bibliolatry, then Baillie is presumably in danger of encouraging the worship of Christians in whom is found the paradox of grace. But Baillie's paradox may still be helpful, as I have outlined above, for our understanding of Scripture. For Scripture is both a divine and a human work. Perhaps when Bible writers recognized the divine origin of their writings, they said, 'Not I, but the grace of God' (see 1 Pet. 1:10–12). An obvious criticism of Baillie is that he has confused the giver of grace (the Lord Jesus) with those who receive that grace (Christian believers). We must maintain that distinction. What then of the Bible? It is a result of God's grace, and we may receive God's grace as we read it. But it is not the giver or origin of grace, as is the Lord Jesus Christ.

If we are to employ analogies to understand the Bible, then, it is perhaps better to use a variety, recognizing the strengths and weaknesses of each of them, but also appreciating that each analogy, though sometimes illuminating, is never complete.

Biblical theology: the Bible as theology

Every preacher has some kind of theology. I believe that the preacher who is ministering on the basis of the three foundations of preaching outlined in Part 1 will be working on the basis of biblical theology. I realize that the term 'biblical theology' can be understood in a variety of ways,[50] but by it I mean 'the theology God teaches us in the Bible'. The quest for biblical theology is of course part of the preparation of any sermon, as we try to understand any text in the context of the whole Bible. I believe that the key features of the biblical-theology approach are the following.

The Bible is God-given. It is common now to view the Bible as a human document in which people of faith grapple as best they can with understanding God. Its function is to inspire us to follow their example (though not their content!), and do the best we can to understand God. I have tried to argue that this view is inadequate, and that some notion of divine as well as human authorship is the only way to do justice to the Bible. The Bible is not just the product of the community of faith; indeed it very often explicitly contradicts, corrects and reforms the faith and practice of the people of God.

This is not to engage in 'bibliolatry', as Moisés Silva points out, but represents an appropriate submission to the God who speaks.[51] Biblical theology is concerned to find out what God is teaching us in the Bible. We look at the complex method of this teaching below.

The Bible is theological. As we have seen, the Bible teaches theology in a whole variety of literary styles. A superficial reading of the Bible will miss most of this theology, if it recognizes theology only in 'theological statements'. But if we are to discover the Bible's meaning, we must be alert to its theology. An untheological reading of the Bible leaves us with only history or psychology.

The merely historical use of the Bible results in attempts to decide what did or did not happen (an exercise popular with both conservative and liberal scholars), without reference to its theological meaning. The Bible is then taught or preached as history, geography, or antiquated social customs. (I well remember a series at school on the missionary journeys of St Paul, which told us a great deal about the geography of the Mediterranean, but nothing about Paul's theology.) Of course the Bible includes history, but it is history with theological meaning.

The psychological approach to Scripture views theological symbols as of merely psychological significance. For example, Jacob's request that his body be taken up from Egypt and buried in Canaan is seen in terms of family loyalty or nostalgia, and not as a firm commitment to God's promise to Abram to give him the land of Canaan (Gn. 49:29–33; 15:7).

The frustrating thing for the preacher is that many modern commentaries are full of information on text, literary context and history, and empty of theology. It is rare to find a modern commentary that tackles the theological meaning of the text, or the theological issues raised by the text. I often resort to Calvin's commentaries to find some theology!

As we shall see, the theology of any part of the Bible needs to be understood in the light of the rest of Scripture, but we must be alert to the theology which is there. There is always the danger of reading theology into a text which gives only background historical information, but there is also the danger of missing out on what God is teaching us in the Bible.

The Bible is self-interpreting. Another insight of biblical theology, consciously practised since the Reformation, is that the Bible is a self-interpreting book; that the key to understanding any part of the Bible will be found elsewhere in the Bible, that any part should be interpreted in the light of the whole, and that subsidiary themes find their right place in the light of major themes. The study of the complex unity of Scripture, of its internal cohesion, was called 'hermeneutics'.[52] This older use of 'hermeneutics', referring to questions of interpretation within Scripture, has now been largely replaced by the modern use, which has to do with the relationship between Scripture and today's world. But the old meaning is of course logically prior to the new. For how can we begin to apply the Bible until we know what it means?

The way in which Scripture is internally self-explanatory is complex, and any theory of its practice needs to take into account its variety of historical and theological settings, the different literary genres, the use of 'intentional heresy' (for instance in the book of Job), the occasions when godly people say less than the truth, and some idea of gradual revelation, of promise and fulfilment. But the Bible's numerous self-quotations in both Testaments are a constant reminder that it is a self-interpreting book.

The fact that the Bible is self-interpreting helps us to make good sense of its diversity and development. Take, for example, the subject of the ministry of the Word. A reading of the Bible that had no room for diversity, development and mutual interpretation would have difficulty in working out which biblical model of the ministry of the Word should be followed by the modern pastor. Should our model be the ecstatic schools of the prophets, the solitary Jeremiah, the disciples of Christ (who travelled around the countryside two by two, casting out demons, healing the sick and preaching the kingdom), or the apostle Paul? Biblical theology helps us to see all of these in context, and to learn from them, but also to recognize that the definitive model for post-apostolic ministry of the Word is described for us in 1 and 2 Timothy and Titus. These epistles depict the kind of ministry to engage in when the apostle is not present, yet it is fully a gospel ministry.

The Bible is cohesive. Biblical theology also asserts the unity of the Bible, and that the Old and New Testaments are mutually illuminating. It also claims that the big themes of the Bible – God's rule, God's covenant, God's grace, God's people, God's plan, God's glory, and the fulfilment of all of these through Jesus Christ – are the continuous message of the Bible from Genesis to Revelation. Biblical theology cannot be happy with the independent development of Old Testament and New Testament theologies.[53] Its aim is to appreciate their distinctive insights, and yet to see how they interpret each other and point to Christ. One of the sad developments of our theological studies is that Old and New Testaments are forced further and further apart, so that the Old Testament is viewed as an exclusively Jewish, not Christian, book. Did Jesus and Paul spend all those hours in the synagogue arguing for a Christian interpretation of the Old Testament in vain? I well remember the great shock I gave a North American ordinand when I reminded him that Jesus thought the Old Testament spoke of himself (Lk. 24:27, 44). We all work with a 'big picture', which helps us interpret the little picture of the text we are grappling with. Biblical theology reminds us that the Bible itself tells us what the 'big picture' is; it is the subject of our preaching: the gospel, Jesus Christ, the whole will of God, the kingdom, and Jesus Christ as Lord.

Every preacher knows that a text out of context is a pretext. Biblical theology reminds us to look not only at the immediate context, but also at the Old or New Testament, and finally at the Bible, as the theological context for every text.

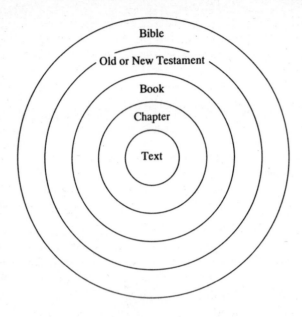

Biblical theology reminds us that the Bible is God-given, theological, self-interpreting and cohesive. It helps us to avoid using the Bible in a 'fundamentalist' way, or a way that is merely historical, psychological, out of context, incoherent or mutually contradictory, or which misuses a minor strand because it has forgotten the big picture. Biblical theology is the preacher's friend.[54]

Is preaching itself the Word of God?

Our topic in this chapter has been *Preach the Word*. Before we finish we tackle the question, 'Is preaching itself the Word of God?'

The issue is raised by the famous statement in the Second Helvetic Confession (1566): 'The preaching of the Word of God is the Word of God' (*praedicatio verbi Dei est verbum Dei*).[55] In the original, these significant words are actually a marginal rubric rather than part of the main body of the text. Nevertheless, as they are original, it seems appropriate to view them as a part of the Confession.[56]

The words which follow this sentence in the Confession do not explain the statement but rather demonstrate its implications. The marginal rubric and the paragraph to which it is appended read as follows:

> The preaching of the Word of God is the Word of God. Where-
> fore when this Word of God is now preached in the church by
> preachers lawfully called, we believe that the very Word of God is
> preached, and received of the faithful; and that neither any other
> Word of God is to be feigned or to be expected from heaven: and
> that now the Word itself which is preached is to be regarded, not
> the minister that preaches; who, although he be evil and a sinner,
> nevertheless the Word of God abides true and good.

The paragraph does not develop the idea that the preaching of the Word of God is in fact the Word of God. The relevant words are *credimus ipsum Dei verbum annunciari et a fidelibus recipi* ('we believe that the very Word of God is preached, and received of the faithful').[57] It is perhaps helpful to notice the context in which this paragraph occurs: the first chapter of the Confession, entitled 'Of the Holy Scripture being the true Word of God'. The chapter begins: 'We believe and confess the Canonical Scriptures of the holy apostles and prophets of both Testaments to be the true Word of God, and to have sufficient authority of themselves, not of men. For God himself spoke to the fathers, prophets, apostles and still speaks to us through the Holy Scriptures.'[58]

Klaas Runia places great emphasis on the idea reflected in the Confession that the preaching of the Word of God is the Word of God. He quotes Luther:

> God, the creator of heaven and earth, speaks with you through
> his preachers, baptises, catechises, absolves you through the
> ministry of his own sacraments. These are the Word of God,
> not of Plato or of Aristotle. It is God Himself who speaks.[59]

Paul Althaus writes:

> The Gospel, however, is nothing else than the preaching and
> proclamation of the grace and mercy of God which Jesus Christ
> has earned and gained for us through his death. It is properly
> not something written down with letters but more an oral
> proclamation and a living Word: a voice which sounds forth
> into the whole world and is proclaimed publicly so that we may
> hear it everywhere.[60]

Luther comments:

> The mouth of the preacher and the Word which I have heard, is
> not his word and preaching, but of the Holy Spirit who through
> such external means gives faith and also sanctifies.[61]

Runia also quotes Calvin, who saw pastors of the Christian church as 'the very mouths of God'. 'When Christ reconciled men to God and to angels, when he conquered the devil and restored life to the dead, when He shone forth with his own righteousness, then indeed God shook the heaven and the earth; and He still shakes them at this day, when the gospel is preached.'[62] Runia then quotes the Helvetic Confession: 'The preaching of the Word of God is the Word of God.' He says that true preaching is not only a matter of human words *about* God; it is the very Word *of* God himself.[63]

Donald Bloesch picks up the same theme from Luther and Calvin. He quotes Luther:

> The Gospel is not really a document, but wishes to be a spoken word, which recites the content of the scripture, just as Christ did not write but only spoke. He did not call his teaching scripture but Gospel, that is, good news or proclamation. That is why it must not be described with the pen but with the mouth . . . Those who are now proclaiming the gospel are not those who really do it; they are only a masquerade through which God carries out his work and will. You are not the ones who are catching the fish, God says, I am drawing the net myself.

Bloesch also quotes Calvin:

> The word goes out from the mouth of God in such a manner that it likewise goes out of the mouth of men; but God does not speak openly from heaven; but employs men as his instruments.[64]

Runia claims that Henry Bullinger's views, reflected in the Helvetic Confession, 'fully represent the view of preaching held by all the Reformers and all the churches of the Reformation'.[65] It may, however, be worth sounding a note of caution and suggesting that the statement 'The preaching of the Word of God is the Word of God' needs some careful theological treatment. As Runia points out, since Bullinger is the author of the Second Helvetic Confession, it is interesting to study his first Decade of sermons, which begins with a series on the Word of God.[66] In his first sermon he takes the topic of its cause and how and by whom it was revealed in the world. In the second sermon he explains that Scripture teaches the whole doctrine of godliness. The first two sermons are thus about the giving of Scripture, but the third is about preaching: 'Of the sense and right exposition of the Word of God, and by what manner of means it may be expounded'. In the light of the famous statement in the Confession, we might expect this third sermon to include an explanation of how the preached word is in reality the Word of God, but none is given. At no point in the third sermon does Bullinger identify the preaching of the Word of God with the Word of God. His exhortation at the end of the second sermon is: 'Let us therefore beseech our Lord God to pour into our minds his holy Spirit, by whose virtue the seed of God's Word may be quickened in our hearts, to the bringing forth of much fruit to the salvation of our souls, and the glory of God our Father.'[67] In the third sermon the argument for the exposition of God's Word is the example given in Scripture of Moses, Jesus and Paul: 'Furthermore, it was a solemn use among the ancient prophets first to read, and then by expositions to apply, God's law to the people. Our Lord Jesus Christ himself expounded the Scriptures. The same did the apostles also. The word of God therefore ought to be expounded . . . for as by the Spirit of God the Scripture was revealed, so by the same Spirit it is requisite to expound it.'[68] Bullinger's argument for the exposition of the Word of God is explained in these words:

> For those which cry out against the exposition of the scriptures, and would not have the ministers of the word and churches to declare the scriptures in open and solemn audience, neither to apply them to the places, times, states and persons, their fetch is to seek somewhat else than the honour due unto God . . . For if a man do read the words of the scripture only, not applying it to the states, places, times and persons, it seemeth that he hath not greatly touched their ungodly and wicked life.[69]

Bullinger's argument here is that sermons are the means by which the Word of God is applied to people, not that the preaching of the Word of God is the Word of God.

The verse often quoted in support of the theory that preaching is the Word of God is 1 Thessalonians 2:13: 'We also constantly give thanks to God for this, that when you received the word of God that you heard from us, you accepted it not as a human word, but as it really is, God's word, which is also at work in you believers.' While this is often taken to be true of all Christian preaching,[70] it might be helpful to see that its primary reference is to the preaching of Paul the apostle. It is very likely that Paul is claiming that his own apostolic words can be described as the Word of God. It may be fair to infer that when we preach Paul's words we are preaching the Word of God, but it does not necessarily follow that our preaching is in itself the Word of God.

This high view of preaching as the Word of God may in fact cause problems. If we begin to understand any one sermon as a Word of God, we are beginning to treat human explanations and ideas as God's words. This looks to me like the beginning of Protestant tradition.

As Runia points out, Karl Barth suggests a way of understanding preaching as the Word of God. Runia summarizes Barth's position as follows:

> As to the Bible, we must begin with a recognition that in itself it is no more than a human witness to God's revelation in Jesus Christ. We must go even further and say: it is not only a human but also a fallible witness, that contains contradictions and errors, even in its religious and theological parts. But how then can we ever hear God's Word in it? Barth's answer is: this is not in our power. Revelation is and always remains a matter of God's prerogative and initiative. Only when and where it pleases God to reveal himself to us through this human and fallible witness, this witness *becomes* the Word of God for us and at that moment *is* the Word of God for us. Only then can we speak of direct identity between the Bible and the Word of God. Or to put it in the terminology of the second Helvetic Confession: only then can we speak of *est* [is]. The same is true of Christian preaching. This too is in itself nothing else than a human attempt to express in human words what the preacher has heard in the apostolic witness and to convey to his hearers the promise of God's revelation, reconciliation and calling . . . the sermon stands under God's own promise that he will use human words to reveal himself. And then we find the same solution: where and when it pleases God to speak through these human words, his self-revelation takes place. At that moment the sermon is God's Word for the hearer.[71]

Runia points out the difficulties with Barth's view:

> The big problem however of Barth's solution is that it does not do justice to Scripture's own testimony about itself, nor to what the New Testament says about the essential nature of preaching. Scripture does not know the Barthian distinction of 'indirect identity' which must become a 'direct identity' where and when it pleases God . . . the New Testament claims that God has revealed himself in Jesus Christ and that this self-revelation for us is to be found in the preaching and writing of the apostles.[72]

Barth's theory may do justice to the freedom of the Spirit at work in the preacher and the hearers, but it does not do justice to the work of God's Spirit in self-revelation through the original giving of the Scriptures.

David Buttrick provides a modern interpretation of the way in which preaching is the Word of God:[73]

> We must modestly claim that preaching is 'the Word of God'
> . . . we believe that through our words God reaches out, claims,
> converts, and saves, because we continue the preaching of Jesus
> Christ . . . Christ transfers preaching to us and gives grace to
> our speaking, so that, odd as it may seem, our sermons are
> Word of God to human communities.[74]

Buttrick argues that our sermons do not become the Word of God by the work of the Spirit bypassing us, for 'grace does not bypass humanity'. His point here seems to be that 'we cannot identify the Spirit with particular rhetoric or particular moments in preaching. The Spirit labours as much in our struggles as in our spontaneities.'[75] Here he is arguing against too glib an association between God using our preaching and moments of exhilaration or excitement. He argues against what he calls a fundamentalist position: 'The repetition of Scripture, or even the careful interpretation of Scripture, does not guarantee that preaching will be Word of God.'[76] Buttrick wants to cut the connection between Scripture and the Word of God in preaching, 'let us be willing to say boldly that it is possible to preach the Word of God without so much as mentioning the Scripture'.[77] He goes on to say that 'an authority model descending from God to Christ through Scripture to sermon could lead to a terrifying arrogance that not only contradicts gospel but destroys preaching'.[78] What Buttrick describes as arrogance may of course represent the humility of accepting God's revelation!

Buttrick's answer to the question, 'How do our words become the Word of God?' is that preachers are chosen: 'We have been *chosen* to speak God's own Word.'[79] It is obvious that this solution is inadequate, as there is no necessary connection between the content of the sermon and God's historical revelation in Jesus Christ.

Walter Brueggemann offers a distinctive interpretation of the role of the preacher. In a prose-flattened world, the preacher comes as poet. The preacher offers 'an evangelical world: an existence shaped by the news of the gospel'.[80] The poet is most like the Old Testament prophet.[81] The strength of Brueggemann's argument lies in his recognition of the preacher's power to evoke a new world of opportunity for the congregation. But he is wrong to claim that this will necessarily exclude 'moral instruction, problem solving or doctrinal clarification'.[82] Perhaps 'the teacher' is a more relevant biblical model than 'the prophet'. And we should remember that vivid and exciting presentation is no guarantee of truth (see 1 Cor. 2:1–5).

What then are we to make of the claim that preaching the Word of God is the Word of God? Though it may be unwise to use 1 Thessalonians 2:13 to support this doctrine, there are other scriptures which may encourage us to adopt this viewpoint. For example, in Romans 10:14 Paul asks: 'How are they to believe in one of whom they have never heard?' The answer is: through preaching. In 2 Corinthians 5:19–20 Paul describes the ministry of the new covenant in these words: 'In Christ God was reconciling the world to himself . . . So we are ambassadors for Christ, since God is making his appeal through us; we entreat you on behalf of Christ, be reconciled to God.' But to claim that Christ may be heard through preaching or that God makes his appeal through preaching is not to claim that the preaching itself is the Word of God.

Perhaps the best way of describing it is to say that when human beings explain the Word of God, preach it, teach it, and urge people to accept it, then the Word of God achieves its purpose, and this is one of the normal ways in which God brings his Word to human beings. It is perhaps helpful to describe this in terms of the work of the Spirit. We must assert that the Spirit was involved in the creation of the Word of God, that is, Scripture. For Scripture is inspired by God (2 Tim. 3:16), and 'no prophecy ever came by human will, but men and women moved by the Holy Spirit spoke from God' (2 Pet. 1:21). We must also recognize the work of the Spirit in the activity of the preacher, and the activity of the Spirit in the minds, hearts and wills of the hearers. The Scripture itself is a product of the Spirit, and when the Spirit works in the preacher and in the hearers, the words of God are mediated and bear fruit in the lives of those who hear.

T. H. L. Parker describes Calvin's view:

> If the preacher faithfully hands on what he himself has learned in the school of God, then God himself 'presides'. He is 'in the midst' as if he were showing himself visibly or face to face, and his people are 'joined' to him. Our Lord Jesus Christ is present and the church is 'united' with him. The pulpit is 'the throne of God from where he wills to govern our souls'. Our responsibility is to 'bear in mind then that the doctrine which we receive of God is as the speech of a King'.[83]

He quotes Calvin again:

> Do we come to the sermon? Is the grace of God presented to us? Are we shown how Jesus Christ has made satisfaction for us, to withdraw us from the curse in which we were? When all that is certified to us it is as good as if the thing itself were presented with us. The reason? When God sends his messengers to announce his will to us he at the same time gives such power that the effect is joined with the Word.[84]

Parker further comments:

We are not to think of preaching as a purely educative exercise and with 'ambassadors for Christ' we are not to consider only a repetition of instructions. This is 'the language of revelation and the activity of the Spirit'. It is not the case that 'God's word needs power to be added to it because in itself it is powerless'. In fact it is the hearer who needs the power in order to become an effectual hearer.[85]

To this we might add that it is the work of the Spirit in the preacher as well as in the hearer that God uses to bring his Spirit-inspired Word to effect in human lives. As Bloesch says in describing Calvin's view: 'God is sovereign even in the preaching of his Word, and his preaching becomes effectual "where it pleases God by the secret power of his Spirit to work in this manner".'[86] Bullinger comments: 'For as by the Spirit of God the Scripture was revealed, so by the same Spirit it is requisite to expound it.'[87]

David Bast discusses the implications of this view of preaching as the means by which the Word of God comes to us.[88] He points out first that 'the preacher's own view of Scripture is of paramount importance. There can be no high view of preaching without a correspondingly high view of Scripture.' It follows, secondly, that 'the nature of preaching is plainly indicated. There are not strictly speaking several kinds of preaching (topical, expository, textual) or many kinds of sermons (doctrinal, lectionary, life situation, relational); there is only one, expositional. The only kind of preaching worthy of the name is that in which the truth of a Scripture text is explained and applied to the lives of the hearers.' Thirdly, 'The task of preaching is clearly defined. The single most important thing the preacher must say to himself each week as he contemplates the sermon lying in front of him is "what am I supposed to be doing?" and the single most specific answer he must repeat is "I am supposed to explain and apply what Scripture says."'[89] Bast goes on to say:

What we who preach need most of all is a commitment to the biblical text. We must not be afraid of the text as if it might spoil our sermon if we spend too much time on it. Let us study it until we can understand and preach what it says, instead of shrinking from it because it doesn't say what we want it to say, or says more than we want it to say. Let us preach the text, not the idea that brought us to the text.[90]

Bast ends his article with a quotation from John Jewel:

Let us persevere with our task and leave the success to the Lord . . . for, as it is our duty to instruct the people with words, so it belongs to God to join to His words faith and force. Such is the power of the Word of God that to effect nothing and to profit no-one is impossible.'[91]

If our preaching is true to Scripture it will be the means by which God brings the Word of God to those who hear us.

In this chapter we have looked at eight issues about the nature of the Bible that affect the preacher. To summarize what we have covered, I list the eight topics, and add to each a brief précis of my recommendations.

The content of Scripture. I encouraged the preacher to teach the gospel, the Word, the message, by means of teaching the Bible. The message is the end, the Bible is the means.

The effectiveness of Scripture. I urged us to believe that God will use Scripture as he has promised, and that he still speaks through its message. The Bible can make us wise for salvation, and train us for ministry. Let us use it!

The nature of Scripture. I claimed that the Bible is propositional, but that it also teaches truth by parable, description, history and sayings. I think that our preaching ought to reflect this variety.

The relevance of Scripture. I want to encourage preachers not to assume the irrelevance of the Bible. A firm theology of God's authorship and purpose for Scripture, and our place in salvation history, will convince us that when Scripture speaks, God speaks.

The use of Scripture. We listed easy ways to misuse Scripture. I encouraged preachers to teach the content of Scripture, use the text for the purpose for which it was written, model a good use of Scripture, and urge our congregations to test what we say by Scripture.

The dual authorship of Scripture. We should respect God's authorship by submitting to his authority, recognizing his presence, believing in his promises and plans in Scripture, and by taking seriously the unity and coherence of the Bible. We should also respect the human authors of Scripture (as God did) by identifying their varied contexts, styles of writing, use of words and place in salvation history. (We also discussed the analogy between Christ and Scripture.)

Biblical theology. We looked at the strength that a preacher can derive from a firm grasp of biblical theology, the belief that the Bible is God-given, theological, self-interpreting, and cohesive. The aim of biblical theology is to get the big message of the Bible right, and to understand each particular part of the Bible in its true biblical and theological context.

Is preaching itself the Word of God? I argued that our preaching conveys the message of God when we preach and teach the words of Scripture.

Notes

1. P. T. Forsyth, *Positive Preaching and the Modern Mind* (London: Independent Press, 1907), p. 6.

2. John Goldingay, *Approaches to Old Testament Interpretation* (Leicester: Apollos, updated edition 1990), p. 152.

3. *Ibid.*, p. 154.

4. Would that all theological colleges and churches shared Paul's conviction about the effectiveness of Scripture in training for Christian ministry!

5. R. E. C. Brown, *The Ministry of the Word* (London: SCM, 1958).

6. *Ibid.*, p. 15.

7. David Buttrick, *Homiletic: Moves and Structures* (London: SCM, 1987), p. 249.

8. Helm, *The Divine Revelation*, pp. 23–25.

9. *Ibid.*, p. 26.

10. Leon Morris, *I Believe in Revelation* (London: Hodder and Stoughton, 1976), p. 114.

11. *Ibid.*, pp. 114–115.

12. J. I. Packer, *'Fundamentalism' and the Word of God* (1958; reissue Leicester: IVP, 1996).

13. Forsyth, *Positive Preaching and the Modern Mind*, p. 6.

14. Gabriel Hebert, *Fundamentalism and the Church of God* (London: SCM, 1957), p. 64.

15. James Barr, *The Bible in the Modern World* (London: SCM, 1973), p. 125.

16. Donald Bloesch, *Essentials of Evangelical Theology* 1 (San Francisco: Harper and Row, 1978), pp. 75–76.

17. *Ibid.*, p. 76.

18. James Smart, *The Strange Silence of the Bible in the Church* (London: SCM, 1970), p. 25.

19. Dennis Nineham, *The Use and Abuse of the Bible* (London: SPCK, 1978).

20. Helm, *The Divine Revelation* p. 48.

21. *Ibid.*

22. *Ibid.*

23. John Stott's excellent chapter on preaching, 'Expounding the Word', in his *The Contemporary Christian* (Leicester and Downers Grove: IVP, 1992) has a useful discussion of 'meaning'; pp. 212–216.

24. Anthony Thiselton, *New Horizons in Hermeneutics* (London: Harper-Collins, 1992), p. 46.

25. John Macquarrie, *Principles of Christian Theology* (London: SCM, 1966), p. 7.

26. *Ibid.*, p. 83.

27. See, *e.g.*, Rom. 15:4; 1 Cor. 10:11.

28. See further Helm, *The Divine Revelation*.

29. Anthony Thiselton, *The Two Horizons* (Exeter: Paternoster, 1980; *idem, New Horizons in Hermeneutics*; and Stott, *The Contemporary Christian*.

30. Greidanus, *The Modern Preacher and the Ancient Text*, pp. 166–167.

31. Augustine, *On Christian Doctrine* (Eng. trans. Edinburgh: T. and T. Clark, 3rd edn 1883), p. 5.

32. I am not competent to discuss the issues of 'meaning' in the light of modern hermeneutical and literary theory. I recommend the following books for starters: Peter Cotterell and Max Turner, *Linguistics and Biblical Interpretation* (London: SPCK, 1989), Elliott E. Johnson, *Expository Hermeneutics: An Introduction* (Grand Rapids: Zondervan, 1990); Tremper Longman III, *Literary Approaches to Biblical Interpretation* (Grand Rapids: Zondervan; Leicester: Apollos, 1987); Moisés Silva, *God, Language and Scripture* (Grand Rapids: Zondervan; Leicester: Apollos, 1990).

33. Packer, *'Fundamentalism' and the Word of God*, p. 80.

34. Packer, *God has Spoken*, pp. 100–101.

35. *Ibid.*, p. 101.

36. *Ibid.*

37. Berkouwer, *Holy Scripture*, p. 199.

38. *Ibid.*

39. *Ibid.*, p. 209.

40. Quoted in Klaas Runia, *Karl Barth's Doctrine of Holy Scripture* (Grand Rapids: Eerdmans, 1962), p. 72.

41. Warfield, *Revelation and Inspiration*, p. 108.

42. Packer, *'Fundamentalism' and the Word of God*, pp. 82–83.

43. Quoted in *ibid.*, p. 82.

44. *Ibid.*, pp. 83–84.

45. D. M. Baillie, *God was in Christ* (London: Faber, 1961).

46. *Ibid.*, p. 114.

47. *Ibid.*, p. 117.

48. *Ibid.*, p. 126.

49. *Ibid.*, p. 129.

50. See, *e.g.*, John Bright, *The Theology of the Old Testament* (Grand Rapids: Baker, 1975), pp. 112–123; Charles Scobie, 'The Challenge of Biblical Theology', Parts 1 and 2, *Tyndale Bulletin* 42.1 and 42.2 (1991), pp. 31–61, 163–194.

51. Silva, *God, Language and Scripture*, p. 38.

52. See, *e.g.*, Milton S. Terry, *Biblical Hermeneutics* (Grand Rapids: Zondervan, 1964).

53. Scobie, 'The Challenge of Biblical Theology', Part 1, pp. 52–53.

54. See Geerhardus Vos, *Biblical Theology* (Edinburgh: Banner of Truth, 1975); Mark Strom, *Days are Coming* (Sydney: Hodder and Stoughton, 1989); Graeme Goldsworthy, *According to Plan* (Leicester: IVP, 1991); William J. Dumbrell, *The End of the Beginning* (Homebush West: Lancer, 1985), Edmund P. Clowney, *Preaching and Biblical Theology* (Phillipsberg: Presbyterian and Reformed, n. d.); *idem*, 'Preaching Christ from all the Scriptures' in Samuel Logan Jr (ed.), *The Preacher and Preaching* (Phillipsberg: Presbyterian and Reformed, 1986); *idem*, *The Unfolding Mystery* (Leicester: IVP, 1988).

55. In John Leith (ed.), *Creeds of the Churches* (Atlanta: John Knox, 1973), p. 133.

56. Klaas Runia, 'What is Preaching according to the New Testament?', p. 35.

57. Philip Schaff, *The Creeds of Christendom* 3 (Grand Rapids: Baker, 1966), p. 237.

58. In Leith (ed.), *Creeds of the Churches*, p. 132.

59. Quoted in Runia, 'What is Preaching . . . ?', p. 33.

60. Quoted in *idem*.
61. Quoted in *idem*.
62. Quoted in *idem*, p. 34.
63. Quoted in *idem*, p. 35.
64. Quoted in Bloesch, *Essentials of Evangelical Theology* 2, p. 75.
65. Runia, 'What is Preaching . . . ?', p. 35.
66. See *The Decades of Henry Bullinger*, ed. Thomas Harding (Cambridge: Cambridge University Press, 1849).
67. *Ibid.*, pp. 69–70.
68. *Ibid.*, p. 74.
69. *Ibid.*, p. 80.
70. Runia, 'What is Preaching . . . ?', p. 35.
71. *Ibid.*, pp. 36–37.
72. *Ibid.*, pp. 37.
73. Buttrick, *Homiletic*, pp. 456ff.
74. *Ibid.*, p. 457.
75. *Ibid.*
76. *Ibid.*
77. *Ibid.*, p. 458.
78. *Ibid.*
79. *Ibid.*, p. 459.
80. Walter Brueggemann, *Finally Comes the Poet* (Minneapolis: Fortress, 1989), pp. 2–3.
81. *Ibid.*, pp. 18ff.
82. *Ibid.*, p. 3.
83. Parker, *Calvin's Preaching*, p. 26.
84. *Ibid.*, p. 28.
85. *Ibid.*, pp. 28–29.
86. Bloesch, *Essentials of Evangelical Theology* 2, p. 76, quoting Calvin's commentary on Isaiah.
87. *The Decades of Henry Bullinger*, p. 80.
88. David M. Bast, 'Why Preach?', *The Reformed Review* 39.3 (Spring 1986), pp. 174ff.
89. *Ibid.*, pp. 175–177.
90. *Ibid.*, pp. 177–178.
91. *Ibid.*, p. 180.

6

The preacher's purpose

In the previous chapters we looked at the three theological foundations of preaching, preaching as a ministry of the Word, and the preacher's Bible. In this chapter we consider the preacher's purpose, the biblical aims of preaching.

The purpose of preaching: the means to an end

As we saw in chapter 3, it is not possible to give a straightforward New Testament answer to the question of the purpose of preaching. The New Testament does not give detailed instructions about what we call preaching (that is, 'the explanation and application of the Word to the congregation of Christ, in order to promote corporate preparation for service, unity of faith, maturity, growth and upbuilding'). Nor does it define preaching. We have seen that it is easy for us to misread the New Testament by reading into its term 'preaching' what we understand by the word. It is possible, however, to answer the question about the purpose of our preaching in terms of the New Testament teaching on ministries of the Word. The New Testament gives us an answer in general terms which we can apply to the particular form of the ministry of the Word with which we are concerned.

The New Testament does not give the answer that 'the purpose of preaching is to preach well'! Many students or preachers have this as their aim. But we have to recognize that this is inadequate and ultimately destructive, because it confuses the means and the end. We can certainly recognize that the ministry of the Word has a place of great importance in God's economy. The preaching or teaching of the Word is not regarded as an end in itself, however, but as a means to an end.

The most helpful way to think of this as we prepare for preaching and as we engage in it is to appreciate that our concentration ought not to be on our preaching or teaching, but on God and Christ and his people. The question is not 'Have I preached well?' but 'Have I served God and Christ and have I served the people of God?' Charles Simeon's questions about a sermon were: 'Does it uniformly tend TO HUMBLE THE SINNER? TO EXALT THE SAVIOUR? TO PROMOTE HOLINESS?'[1]

We can see from many examples in the New Testament that preaching is not an end in itself, but a means to an end, and that the concentration of the minister of the Word must always be on God and Christ and his people. This is evident in the Great Commission: 'Go therefore and make disciples of all nations, baptizing them in the name of the Father and of the Son and of the Holy Spirit, and teaching them to obey everything that I have commanded you. And remember, I am with you always, to the end of the age' (Mt. 28:19–20). We should notice that baptizing and teaching are means to an end. The end or purpose of the teaching is to make disciples of all nations. We notice the same point in Paul's explanation of his ministry in 2 Corinthians: 'By the open statement of the truth we commend ourselves to the conscience of everyone in the sight of God' (4:2). The purpose of setting forth the word plainly, then, is to commend the apostolic message and to minister to the conscience of every hearer in the sight of God. Paul again summarizes his ministry in Colossians: 'It is he whom we proclaim, warning everyone and teaching everyone in all wisdom, so that we may present everyone mature in Christ' (1:28). Again Paul's ministry is focused on Christ and his aim is to present his hearers mature in Christ.

The strength of John Stott's definition of preaching in *The Contemporary Christian* is its clear statement of intentionality. 'To preach is to open up the inspired text with such faithfulness and sensitivity that God's voice is heard and God's people obey him.'[2] Preaching is not an end in itself. It is, to make the obvious point, a form of Christian ministry through which we serve God and Christ, the Word of God, and the people of God.

In this chapter we shall consider the threefold purpose of preaching: we serve God and Christ, we serve the Word of God, and we serve the people of God.

Serving God and Christ

We serve God and Christ in our preaching as we are true to God, his purpose for preaching and his call to us to be servants of his Word and of his people. We are servants of God as we recognize God as the author of Scripture, and as the one who speaks now through Scripture which is his voice, his preaching, his sermon. We serve God in our ministry of the Word also as we recognize that as we exercise our ministry God is present, working and active.

Notice the manifold work of God described by Paul in 2 Thessalonians 2:13–17.

> But we must always give thanks to God for you, brothers and sisters beloved by the Lord, because *God chose you* as the firstfruits for salvation *through sanctification by the Spirit* and

through belief in the truth. For this purpose *he called you through* our *proclamation of the good news,* so that you may obtain the glory of our Lord Jesus Christ. So then, brothers and sisters, stand firm and hold fast to the *traditions that you were taught by us,* either by word of mouth or by our letter. Now *may our Lord Jesus Christ himself and God our Father, who loved us and through grace gave us eternal comfort and good hope, comfort your hearts and strengthen them in every good work and word.*

God chose the Christians at Thessalonica to be saved. His choice was implemented through the sanctifying work of the Spirit and through their belief in the truth of the gospel. God is the one who called the Thessalonians to believe in the truth of the gospel that Paul and his friends preached, and God's aim was that the Thessalonians might obtain the glory of the Lord Jesus Christ. As the Thessalonians stand firm and hold to the teachings that were passed on to them by Paul and his friends, whether by word of mouth or by letter, God does his part. As they stand firm, Paul's prayer is that our Lord Jesus Christ himself and God our Father would comfort their hearts and strengthen them in every good work and word. The apostle has a vivid sense of God working as he engages in his ministry.

I am emphasizing this element of New Testament teaching because I think that occasionally those who have a firm trust in the God-given nature of Scripture minister in a way which is functionally deistic, with the belief that God has set up the world according to a certain pre-arranged pattern and that all we have to do is to recognize it and act accordingly. When people adopt this view of God they function as deists, believing that they must do all the work and that God is absent or inactive.

Paul is confident that God is at work in his own ministry. 'For this I toil and struggle with all the energy that he powerfully inspires within me' (Col. 1:29). It is therefore appropriate for Paul to ask for prayer for his ministry: 'Finally, brothers and sisters, pray for us, so that the word of the Lord may spread rapidly and be glorified everywhere, just as it is among you, and that we may be rescued from wicked and evil people; for not all have faith' (2 Thes. 3:1–2). Again, 'I appeal to you, brothers and sisters, by our Lord Jesus Christ and by the love of the Spirit, to join me in earnest prayer [lit. struggle with me in prayer] to God on my behalf' (Rom. 15:30). Paul's association of the notion of struggle with prayer means that he is requesting not a token prayer but a significant participation in the work of God through Paul.

If we are to serve God in our ministry of preaching we must respect God, his words and his people, believe that God is going to work through our Christian ministry, and pray that he will do so. To be servants of God and of Christ in our ministry also means that ultimately we are answerable for our ministry to God alone (1 Cor. 4:4).

Serving the Word of God

Our serving of the text may not necessarily be in preaching (that is, in a formal, public monologue), but may take one of the many and varied forms of ministry of the Word. If we preach as one of those forms, our preaching certainly needs to be exegetical, concerned with teaching the content, and explaining the meaning, of a part of Scripture.

This does not necessarily mean that we engage all the time in expository preaching (that is, preaching our way through a book of the Bible verse by verse or chapter by chapter). There are good arguments for engaging in this kind of ministry. It helps people to get a wide view of the Word of God, and to understand texts in context; and it gives them a good model of Bible reading. It also encourages people to take the Bible seriously. Yet the New Testament does not explicitly direct us to this form of preaching. It encourages us to engage in our ministry of the Word but does not tell us how to do it. The arguments for expository preaching are theological and pragmatic rather than based upon direct instructions from Scripture.

I believe that we need to restore good models of expository preaching as the staple diet of our Sunday sermons. Here are some reasons for preaching expository sermons.

First, expository sermons help us to let God set the agenda for our lives. The danger of topical preaching is that it implies that we know what is important! Expository preaching lets God set the agenda in an obvious and public way.

Secondly, expository preaching treats the Bible as God treated it, respecting the particular contexts, history and style of the human authors. God chose to have the Bible written in books, each by a human author, and not as a collection of useful but disconnected sayings. We should follow God by preaching the way he wrote.

Thirdly, this kind of preaching gives ample time for us to make clear the context of the Bible passage from which we are preaching. If the Bible passage follows on from last week, the congregation will understand the context clearly. If I change the context each week, and include three or four Bible passages in my sermon, it will be very hard for the congregation to hear any text in context. This is not a model we should encourage. Expository preaching helps us to take each text in context, as God caused it to be written.[3]

It is sobering to notice why the fine expository preaching tradition of the early church, as found, for example, in Augustine and John Chrysostom, died out. One reason was that theological controversy often reduced sermons to political point-scoring rather than serious explanation of the text. Immediate and urgent needs prevailed. Another was the large number of people ignorant of the Christian faith. This meant that sermons had to become more immediately accessible. A further factor was the increasing concentration on liturgy, which meant that there was less time available to preach. Finally, low standards of training for clergy meant that many were unable to preach biblical sermons.[4] Are these some of the pressures against expository preachers today?

In my own view the bulk of our preaching ought to be expository, and it is good to get a balance between Old and New Testament books and different styles of books within the Bible. For many people this is the basic form of Christian teaching and preaching. What I call expository sermons move clearly from 'text' to 'today'.

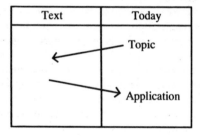

Of course, good topical preaching is still exegetical. A topical sermon begins with a topic of current relevance, goes to the Bible to discover a godly way of responding, and then encourages that practical response.

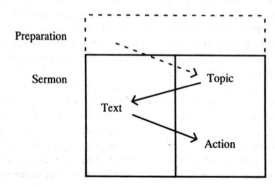

Behind the scenes, the way the preacher thinks about a topic, and raises it in the sermon, will also be informed by the Bible.

If the preacher is thinking biblically, then, the sermon will be exegetical, both because his search for the topic is from a biblical perspective, and because, having raised the topic in the sermon, he then goes to the Bible to find out how we should respond. This kind of preaching requires a very good understanding of the Bible, careful choice of key passages, a clear perception of how the Bible interacts with the topic in question, and great skill in applying the chosen texts in context. The advantage of moving from a current issue to Scripture is that it encourages people to think Christianly and biblically about their lives and the issues that they meet each day. Lay people, and indeed most Christian workers, do not live through an exegesis of (say) Ephesians; rather, we meet issues in daily life and wonder what the Bible says about them. If for no other reason, therefore, topical or issue preaching provides a helpful model for Christian living. Yet it must be said that this approach is very difficult for the preacher. It is difficult to avoid being superficial about both the topic and the Bible, and in my experience it takes twice as much preparation as an expository sermon.

Serving the people of God

If we are servants of God and of Christ, and servants of his Word, then the call of the preacher is also to be a servant of God's people. In Colossians, immediately after Paul has described himself as a servant of the gospel, he describes himself as a servant of the church to make the Word of God fully known (1:23–25). Paul's relationship to his hearers is not one of remote academic isolation (a model of teaching which is now powerful in the West and is a product of Enlightenment thinking about autonomy, free enquiry and independence). Paul continually describes himself as being in the closest relationship with those to whom he ministers. 'I am not writing this to make you ashamed, but to admonish you as my beloved children. For though you may have ten thousand guardians in Christ, you do not have many fathers. Indeed, in Christ Jesus I became your father through the gospel' (1 Cor. 4:14–15). 'We were gentle among you, like a nurse tenderly caring for her own children. So deeply do we care for you that we are determined to share with you not only the gospel of God but also our own selves, because you have become very dear to us' (1 Thes. 2:7–8). This is the language of deep personal commitment, indicating the style of servanthood and service Paul has in mind.

Notice how Paul balances giving instructions with making an emotional appeal. 'We ask you and urge you in the Lord Jesus that, as you learned from us how to live and to please God . . . you should do so more and more. For you know what instructions we gave you through the Lord Jesus' (1 Thes. 4:1–2). We sometimes see Paul as characteristically issuing commands and instructions, but he is equally happy to appeal, ask and urge (see also 1 Thes. 5:12, 14). If the language of instruction and command is that of a superior to an inferior, Paul also uses the language of asking and urging in which he opens his heart of love to them.

In chapter 3 we observed in the ministries of Moses and Ezra the three elements of exposition, application and exhortation, as they explained the truth, applied it to their hearers and urged them to respond. The same threefold pattern was evident in Peter's sermon on the day of Pentecost. Again, we have found this pattern in Paul and Hebrews, where the truth is explained and applied to the readers, and they are urged to respond. We have seen also that the word 'exhortation' or 'encouragement' (*paraklēsis*), used in Acts 13:14ff. and Hebrews 13:22, includes these three elements. Would we be wise to drop the words 'preach', 'preacher' and 'sermon' to describe our Sunday-by-Sunday activity, substituting 'encourage', 'encourager' and 'encouragement'?

For Paul, the ministry of the Word embraces not only what we call exegesis but also application and exhortation. It includes not only an intellectual or conceptual explanation of the content of the message, but also practical instructions about its impact on his hearers or readers, and an emotional appeal to respond in appropriate ways. To those who are committed to the idea that the ministry of the Word consists of solid exegesis, my point is that solid exegesis alone is not enough, and that the ministry of the Word, and in particular preaching, must also include practical instruction or application and an exhortation or emotional appeal to the hearers to respond. We, like Paul, must serve our people.

I find that a useful way to achieve this is to work on a *ministry sentence* for every sermon. A ministry sentence is a summary of the sermon, its main point. It summarizes my ministry to the congregation, is expressed in terms of the expected response, and includes an element of appeal or challenge. It is characteristically expressed in terms of doing, rather than just knowing. If my sermon is on 1 Corinthians 6:12–20, for instance, I do not just want people to know that sexual immorality is wrong. I want them to run away from it! My ministry sentence, the focus and purpose of my sermon, is 'Flee immorality!' In a sermon on Galatians 4:12 – 5:1, it is 'Stand firm in freedom!' My ministry sentence helps me to focus my sermon, and helps my hearers to know what the sermon is about. It is a call, an appeal, to action and response. I settle on the ministry sentence (and it takes a long time!) by asking myself: 'What is God saying to this congregation through this text?' and 'What response does he want them to make?' A ministry sentence helps me to apply the teaching.

In so far as the Bible is itself a model of the ministry of the Word we must notice that in every case the message is applied. Runia writes:

The New Testament writings were not religious tracts in which the doctrine of God's salvation in Jesus Christ was expounded in a purely objective way, but occasional writings, prompted by a particular situation in the community and seeking to evaluate this situation in the light of God's saving action in Jesus Christ. This is quite obvious in the case of Paul's letters. Every letter is an occasional writing prompted by the situation of the congregation concerned. In each case the apostle deals explicitly with the situation and expounds the gospel of Jesus Christ in such a way that the situation is really illuminated by the gospel either positively or negatively.[5]

In this way true preaching will reflect the nature of Scripture which is not a monologue but rather a dialogue between God and his people. Runia concludes:

Scripture itself teaches us that God speaking to his people is always dialogical in its very nature. God's revelation to his people is never a proclamation of some abstract, purely objective truth, but God always reveals himself into their active situation. Thus the Old Testament prophets always addressed the people in their concrete historical circumstances. So too, Paul always expounded the significance of the cross and resurrection of Christ in direct relation to the actual needs of his congregations.[6]

The dialogue within the sermon will involve expressing both God's words and the congregation's words. God's words are found in the Bible; the congregation's words will be found deep in their lives and hearts. We need to listen well to hear them. As Walter Brueggemann has demonstrated, good preaching ensures that this real dialogue takes place.[7] The value of reader-response study of Scripture is that it helps us to articulate one side of the dialogue (that of the congregation), and that this helps us to hear the other side, if it does not deafen us by its strong demands.

Calvin too places great emphasis on the work of the preacher in applying the message of Scripture to his hearers.

What advantage would there be if we were to stay here half a day and I were to expound half a book without considering you or your profit and edification? . . . We must take into consideration those persons to whom the teaching is addressed . . . For this reason let us note well that they who have this charge to teach, when they speak to a people, are to decide which teaching will be good and profitable so that they will be able to disseminate it faithfully and with discretion to the usefulness of everyone individually.[8]

For most of us, however, it is not that we have a theological objection to using the Bible to correct, rebuke and encourage, or that we do not want to apply it, but that we find it hard to do. The sermon which ends with the prayer, '. . . and may God show us how to put this into practice in our everyday lives', is the sermon of a preacher who does not know how it should be applied. In such a case I suspect that the people will remain in ignorance too. How can we help ourselves to work on application? In the next section of this chapter we shall look at the Puritans, and the great lessons they can teach us on how to apply Scripture to our hearts. But first, here are my own suggestions.

Ask: 'what message does God want to give these people from this text?'

Focus upon four or five representative people in your congregation (one old, one young, one single, one married, one male, one female, *etc.*) and think through what difference you want this text to make to their lives.

Work out the main ideas, preconceptions, movements, and theological strands in the congregation, and apply the text to each of them (the conservatives, the charismatics, the progressives, *etc.*).

Meet once a week with various members of the congregation, talk with them about the text you plan to preach on next Sunday, and ask them what they make of it.

Meet every Monday night with a small group to discuss the sermon you preached yesterday, and the text you will preach on next Sunday.

Imagine you are counselling an individual. How would you apply this text to that person?

Pray for your people more, and learn to love them more. Love is quick-eyed.

Spend only half your preparation time on the meaning of the text, and then spend the rest of the time working on the application.

Finally, make use of the 'text and today' boxes in your preparation, to help you in application.

Text	Today
1 2 The 3 points 3 of the text	Application to today

A common pattern is to preach the sermon, then add the application.

Text	Today
1	
2	
3	
⟶	Application

This is not a bad approach, but it has some drawbacks. If used every week, it will become boring; it encourages people to slumber for most of the sermon, and wake up for the last five minutes; and if the preacher runs out of time, then the application is rushed or left out.

Another method is to apply the points of the sermon on the way through.

Text	Today
1 ⟶	Application
2 ⟶	Application
3 ⟶	Application
Summary ⟶	Summary

This encourages people to listen, and each relevant application prompts close attention to the next point from the text.

Another way of preaching is to begin with the confusion and misunderstanding that surround us today on the subject of the text, go to the text for the truth, and then apply the truth to the congregation.

Text	Today
Text	Wrong ideas and practice
	Right ideas and practice

I think it is good to vary the way in which we move between text and application, and also to be conscious of what we are doing. Using these 'text and today' boxes as part of our method of preparation also helps us to see if we have any application to make! Remember that application is not our artificial imposition on the text, but the answer to the question, 'What is God teaching his people through this text?'

Learning from the Puritans

We have looked at some practical suggestions on how to work on application. We can also find much to help us in the preaching style of the Puritans, who excelled in the science of application.[9] J. I. Packer claims that 'the theory of discriminating application is the most valuable legacy that Puritan preachers have left to those who would preach the Bible and its gospel effectively today'.[10] We serve God, the text, and our people when we bring home God's message in the Bible to their hearts, minds and lives. We can begin with the vigorous theology of preaching of William Perkins (1558–1602), and his recognition of the need of 'special application'.

> First of all, the hearing of the Word of God preached by the ministry of man is an ordinance of God . . . ordained and founded by God himself in Mt. Sinai. This ordinance Christ renewed when he said 'the scribes and pharisees sit in Moses' chair; hear them' (Matt. 23:1) and that this ordinance must so continue to the end of the world the prophet Isaiah teacheth (Isa. 2:3). Secondly the preaching and hearing of the Word of God is a common and usual means of God to begin and confirm faith and all graces of God that depend on faith and consequently to work out our salvation (Rom. 1:16–18; 10:14; 1 Cor. 1:21). That we may be saved we must have special faith: special faith requires a special Word and the written word being otherwise general is made special by application: and this application is effectually made by the ministry of the Word in which men called thereto apply particularly to the consciences of their hearts the commandments and promises of God and that in the name of God.[11]

Perkins was so convinced of the need to train people in preaching, and in helping them in the art of special application, that he wrote *The Art of Prophecy* (or *A treatise concerning the sacred and only true manner and method of Preaching first written by Mr William Perkins*). 'The art or faculty of prophesying is a sacred doctrine of exercising prophecy rightly. Prophecy (or prophesying) is a public and solemn speech of the prophet pertaining to the worship of God and the salvation of our neighbour.'[12]

Perkins placed high value on 'rightly dividing' or rightly applying the

Word. '*Of the right dividing of the Word*. Hitherto we have spoken of interpreting of the Word. We now come to speak of the right cutting or the right dividing of it. The right cutting of the Word is that whereby the Word is made fit to edify the people of God.'[13] Because of the priority of correct and edifying application which, in Perkins's words, is 'that whereby the Doctrine rightly collected is diversely fitted as place, time and person do require (Ezek. 34:15–16; Jude 22–23)',[14] he worked out a sevenfold system of application to the varied needs of members of his congregation.

> The ways of application are chiefly seven according the divers condition of men and people which is sevenfold.
> I.   Unbelievers who are both ignorant and unteachable . . .
> II. Some are teachable, but yet ignorant . . .
> III. Some have knowledge, but are not as yet humbled . . .
> IV. Some are humbled . . .
> V.   Some do believe . . .
> VI. Some are fallen . . .
> VII. There is a mingled people . . .[15]

The rigorous use of this method of thinking about application in our congregations would at least save us from always preaching at the same level of understanding and faith. We can address different points in the sermon to different groups; we could name them ('I am relating this to those of you who have fallen away . . .'). We should notice that this science of careful application did not originate with the Puritans. We find Augustine of Hippo writing:

> It will likewise make a considerable difference, even when we are discoursing in that style, whether there are few present or many, whether they are learned or unlearned, or made up of both classes combined; whether they are city-bred or rustics, or the one and the other together, or whether again, they are a people composed of all orders of men in due proportion . . . I find myself variously moved, according as I see before me, for the purposes of catechetical instruction, a highly educated man, a dull fellow, a citizen, a foreigner, a rich man, a poor man, a private individual, a man of honours, a person occupying some position of authority, an individual of this or the other nation, of this or the other age or sex, one proceeding from this or the other sect, from this or the other common error . . . although the same charity is due to all yet the same medicine is not to be administered to all.[16]

Of course, if the preacher who tries to follow this example of applicatory preaching also engages in Richard Baxter's model of close and effective pastoral care of the congregation (see chapter 4), then he or she will have that intimate knowledge of the people necessary for specific application to different classes of hearer.

The Westminster *Directory for the Public Worship of God* urges the preacher to engage in effective application:

> He is not to rest in general doctrine, although never so much cleared and confirmed, but to bring it home to special use, by application to his hearers: which albeit prove a great work of difficulty to himself, requiring much prudence, zeal, and meditation, and to the natural and corrupt man will be very unpleasant; yet he is to endeavour to perform it in such a manner, that his auditors may feel the word of God to be quick and powerful, and a discerner of the thoughts and intent of the heart; and that, if any unbeliever or ignorant person be present, he may have the secrets of his heart made manifest, and give glory to God.[17]

We have been discussing the purpose of preaching in terms of being servants of God and of Christ, servants of his Word and servants of his people. If we do all this, then we will be productive in that ministry which we have described as 'the explanation and application of the Word of God to the congregation of Christ, in order to promote corporate preparation for service, unity of faith, maturity, growth, and upbuilding'.

John Calvin's theology of preaching[18]

We now turn again to study the ministry of John Calvin, where we will see these priorities of preaching illustrated in a disciplined, passionate and effective way.

We have already outlined Calvin's varied ministry of the Word in chapter 4, focusing on his writing, public speaking, church discipline and pastoral ministry to individuals. We now concentrate on Calvin the preacher, perhaps less well known than Calvin the writer, but of great interest to us. Not only was Calvin's preaching ministry markedly effective among those who heard him (especially visitors and exiles resident in Geneva), but his published sermons had a great impact on his contemporaries who were engaged in the ministry of preaching. It would be foolish to reproduce Calvin's preaching in our congregations today, but it is very instructive to learn from his theology and practice of preaching.

The key to these lies in his deep understanding that God *accommodates* himself to our weakness.[19] Of course, the main way in which God accommodates to our weakness is in the coming of his Son, the Lord Jesus Christ. 'In Christ God so to speak makes himself little, in order to lower himself to our capacity; and Christ alone calms our consciences that they may dare intimately approach God.'[20] God's accommodation to us is also found in the way in which he speaks to us in Scripture, in his preachers and teachers, and in the Holy Spirit. It is in the context of this theology of God's accommodating himself to us in order to speak to us that we find Calvin's theology of preaching.

God and Scripture
God accommodates himself to us in Scripture.

> How did Calvin regard Holy Scripture? . . . His concept of Scripture focused on two related ideas. The first is *os Dei*, the mouth of God – that is, God's use of human language to address us. The second is *doctrina*, teaching – that is, instruction conveyed by God's verbal utterances. 'Teaching from the mouth of God' or more simply and dynamically 'God speaking', 'God teaching' or 'God preaching', is the essence of Calvin's view of Scripture.[21]

God's speaking to us in Scripture accommodates to our weakness.

> For who even of slight intelligence does not understand that, as nurses commonly do with infants, God is wont in a measure to 'lisp' in speaking to us? Thus such forms of speaking do not so much express clearly what God is like as accommodate the knowledge of him to our slight capacity. To this he must descend far beneath his loftiness.[22]

> But as Scripture, having regard for men's rude and stupid wit, customarily speaks in the manner of the common folk, where it would distinguish the true God from the false it particularly contrasts him with idols.[23]

> God spoke in a gross and uncultured manner and sought to accommodate himself to the great and the small and the less intelligent.[24]

> But, it is most stupid not to honour the Word of God, because he has lowered himself to the level of our ignorance. When we find God prattling to us in the Bible in an uncultivated and vulgar style let us remember that he does it for our sake. Anyone who presumes or pretends to be offended by the

condescension of God so that he will not submit to God's Word, is a liar. Anyone who cannot bear to lay hold of God as he comes down to him will still less soar up to him beyond the clouds . . . for even though Christ's discourse as a whole was heavenly, he spoke plainly as it were in an *earthly* way. Furthermore this is not true of one discourse only. In this verse Christ's habitually simple and popular way of teaching is contrasted with ambitious men's addiction to speech that is full of pomp and splendour.[25]

The first stage in God's accommodating himself to us in speaking to us, then, is Scripture, where he speaks in plain human language to our weakness.

God and the preacher

God has accommodated to us in our weakness by providing us not only with Scripture but also with preachers and teachers. Calvin gives a number of reasons for this. First, God himself is invisible.

Nevertheless, because he does not dwell among us in visible presence . . . we have said that he uses the ministry of men to declare openly his will to us by mouth, as a sort of delegated work, not by transferring to them his right and honour, but only that through their mouths he may do his own work just as a workman uses a tool to do his work.[26]

For, among the many excellent gifts with which God has adorned the human race, it is a singular privilege that he deigns to consecrate to himself the mouths and tongues of men in order that his voice may resound in them.[27]

Secondly, God shows his regard for human beings.

For by this means he first declares his regard for us when from among men he takes some to serve as his ambassadors in the world, to be interpreters of his secret will and, in short, to represent his person.[28]

Thirdly, it teaches people humility.

Again, this is the best and most useful exercise in humility, when he accustoms us to obey his Word, even though it be preached through men like us and sometimes by those of lower worth than we . . . when a puny man risen from the dust speaks in God's name, at this point we best evidence our piety and obedience toward God if we show ourselves teachable towards his minister although he excels us in nothing.[29]

Fourthly, it fosters mutual love.

Nothing fosters mutual love more fittingly than for men to be bound together with this bond: one is appointed pastor to teach the rest, and those bidden to be pupils receive the common teaching from one mouth.[30]

Fifthly, the use of ministers is a way in which God proves our obedience.

As he was of old not content with the law alone, but added priests as interpreters from whose lips the people might ask its true meaning, so today he not only desires us to be attentive to its reading, but also appoints instructors to help us by their effort . . . he proves our obedience by a very good test when we hear his ministers speaking just as if he himself spoke.[31]

Sixthly, he accommodates to our weakness.

He also provides for our weakness in that he prefers to address us in human fashion through interpreters in order to draw us to himself, rather than to thunder at us and drive us away.[32]

God condescends to our weakness, then, in sending preachers and teachers of his Word:

We have already seen how God, having respect to our frailty, has vouchsafed to use this way to draw us to himself, that is, that we should be taught in homely fashion by mortal men like ourselves, and in this he also shows that he had an eye to what might be fittest for his own. For in saying that he will always send a Prophet in Israel from among the people (Dt. 18:18; Jn. 1:45) he intended to show that we did not need to seek him far, but that he would find a way to commune familiarly with us. Therefore when the gospel is preached among us, God's applying himself in that way to our weakness is as much as if he came down to us himself . . . how greatly he loves us in that he deals with us according to our own small capacity.[33]

Finally, God speaks with a living voice. But it is still God who speaks to us by this humble means. 'Wherever the gospel is preached, it is as if God himself came into the midst of us'.[34] For God delights to speak with a living voice. 'God would ever have the living voice to resound in His Church . . . nowadays preaching is inseparably united with Scripture.'[35]

Thus God accommodates himself in this way to our weakness. But how does this work in practical ways in preaching and teaching? What are the special weaknesses of human beings that preachers should keep in mind? And how should God's accommodation to our hearers be expressed in our preaching? The answers to these questions are found most powerfully and movingly in Calvin's sermons on Timothy and Titus. The language is antiquated; the issues are contemporary.

> What was said to us in the last sermon was to stir up every one of us to read the Holy Scripture, seeing it is so profitable to us, and God has included in it whatsoever is requisite to our salvation. But yet God did not content himself to put forth the Holy Scripture that every man might study it, but he devised of his infinite goodness a second means to instruct us; he would have the doctrine that is therein contained preached and expounded to us. And for this end and purpose he has appointed shepherds in his church which have the office and charge of teaching. This aid God thought good to add because of our slowness. It was already very much that he had given us his word and caused it to be written that every one of us might read it and learn it. God showed himself herein very liberal toward us. But when we see he deals with us after our weakness and chews our morsels for us that we might digest them the better, in that he feeds us as little children, we shall never be able to excuse ourselves, unless we profit in his school.[36]

God chews up our food for us, by providing us with preachers, so that we can more easily digest his words to us in Scripture. What a great picture of God's compassion! What a challenge to the preacher!

And our preaching must be passionate!

> St. Paul shows that it is not enough to preach the law of God and the promises and what else is contained in Holy Scripture as though a man should teach in a school. But we must 'improve, threaten and exhort'. If we leave it to men's choice to follow that is taught them, they will never move one foot. Therefore the doctrine of itself can profit nothing at all unless it be confirmed by exhortations and by threats, unless there be spurs to prick men withall. For like beasts that are so wild and

fierce, if they should be let alone to lie grovelling in their slothfulness, it will be hard to make them profit in the end and to go on in the way of salvation.[37]

Mere teaching without exhortation is pointless.

The word 'exhort' or 'warn' imports that we should be wakened up from our slothfulness. For we see that if a man do no more than expound the Holy Scripture it slips away, and we be not touched to the quick. Therefore if teaching be not helped with exhortations it is cold and pierces not our hearts.[38]

The preacher is like a surgeon searching out a wound.

But we must moreover be quickened up with good and vehement exhortations; we must be rebuked as if a man should search a wound. For as much as our diseases are most commonly secret, God must be feign to enter them and go even to the very marrow of the bones, as the apostle says in the Epistle to the Hebrews, so that there may be neither thought nor affection but every whit of it be searched to the bottom by God's word.[39]

Preachers must, then, have truth and passion.

Therefore there are two things requisite, that is that we give good and sound understanding of what is requisite for the salvation of the faithful, and then that we add there withall a vehemency to the end that the doctrine may touch their hearts to the quick, and, they not only know what is good but be moved to follow it. Therefore the two things that are here joined together (doctrine and exhortation) may in no wise be sundered.[40]

Indeed, God accommodates himself so completely to the theological, emotional and spiritual needs of his people through his preachers that a sermon is always specially directed to the particular congregation in which it is preached. God accommodates himself to your congregation through you, the preacher! Badius, Calvin's contemporary and publisher, points out that Calvin was reluctant to have his sermons published, because they were specifically directed to his congregation at Geneva. 'He desired that his sermons should not extend further than his pastorate; because they were preached especially for his sheep, to whose capacity he accommodated himself as best he could.'[41]

This ability to preach directly to the congregation, to apply the Word of God, Calvin describes as a gift of prophecy. 'Prophets are (1.)

outstanding interpreters of Scripture; and (2.) men endowed with extraordinary wisdom and aptitude for grasping what the immediate need of the Church is, and speaking the right word to meet it.'[42] And so, 'We ought to imitate the Prophets, who conveyed the doctrine of the Law in such a manner as to draw from it advices, reproofs, threatening and consolations which they applied to the present condition of the people.'[43]

When he published Calvin's sermons on the Ten Commandments, Badius wrote of Calvin's ministry:

> Among the most excellent gifts with which God has enriched his Church in all times, one of the most useful and necessary is that of Prophecy. It exists for the purpose of clearly under-standing and purely expounding to God's people the Holy Scripture according to its *vray et naturel sens* (true and natural sense) and of understanding how to apply it properly to one's own time and in accordance with those with whom one has to do . . . I thought that I would bring to the people a great consolation through the use of my art by enabling them to behold that pasture which sustains us and in what simplicity, purity, truth, reverence and zeal the Word of God is proclaimed to us by those whom the Lord Jesus has commissioned as Pastors over his flock in this country.[44]

Through such prophetic preaching God works in a profound way in the congregation that hears a sermon. Calvin says:

> It is certain that if we come to church we shall not hear only a mortal man speaking but we shall feel (even by his secret power) that God is speaking to our souls, that he is the teacher. He so touches us that the human voice enters into us and so profits us that we are refreshed and nourished by it.[45]

> He [God] calls us to him as if he had his mouth open and we saw him there in person.[46]

God and his Spirit

We have seen that God accommodates his words to us in Scripture and in his preachers and teachers. The third way in which God accommodates to our weakness is that he sends his Holy Spirit to confirm the truth that he has revealed.

> The Word itself is not quite certain for us unless it be confirmed by the testimony of the Spirit . . . God did not bring

forth his Word among men for the sake of a momentary display, intending at the coming of his Spirit to abolish it. Rather he sent down the same Spirit by whose power he had dispensed the Word, to complete his work by the efficacious confirmation of the Word.[47]

God works in his elect in two ways: within, through his Spirit; without, through his Word. By this Spirit, illuminating their minds and forming their hearts to the love and cultivation of righteousness, he makes them a new creation. By his Word, he arouses them to desire, to seek after and attain that same renewal. In both he reveals the working of his hand according to the mode of dispensation.[48]

It is therefore by the work of the Spirit that God brings his Word to us.

Besides, since Christ testified that it was the peculiar office of the Holy Spirit to teach the apostles whom he himself had already taught by word of mouth, it follows that outward preaching is vain and useless unless the Spirit himself acts as the teacher. God therefore teaches in two ways. He makes us hear his voice through the words of men, and inwardly he constrains us by his Spirit.[49]

But let it be clear that he is speaking here not of the secret revelation but of the power of the Spirit which is manifested in the external teaching of the gospel, and that by the voice of men.[50]

The congregation too needs to be taught by God's Holy Spirit.

When we come to hear the sermon or take up Holy Scripture to read it, let us not have this foolish presumption of thinking that we shall easily understand by our own wit everything that is said to us and that we read; but let us come with reverence, waiting entirely on God, well aware that we have need to be taught by his Holy Spirit, and that without that we can in no way understand what is shown us in his Word.[51]

Calvin refers to this secret working of God's Holy Spirit.

For we all of us have one general creation by which we live in this world, but God creates us new again when he vouchsafes to give us newness of life by his gospel. I mean when he prints it in our hearts and minds by his own secret working, for the Word alone would not be enough to do it.[52]

The members of the congregation know that when they hear God speaking to them during the sermon it is because God himself is present in the means he has appointed, and because he has come down to them, accommodated himself to their weakness in his words of Scripture, in the ministry of the preacher, and through the work of the Holy Spirit.

And what of the preacher?

First, the preacher must ensure that he or she is speaking and teaching the words of God in Scripture, that God's truths are being taught and heard. Since Scripture is the 'mouth of God', when the preacher teaches the truth of God from the Scriptures, God's voice will be heard in the preacher's words; he or she will be God's mouthpiece, with the great privilege of speaking God's words.

Secondly, the preacher must be aware that he or she is called by God to be the way in which God accommodates himself to that particular congregation. The preacher is part of God's coming down to the level of the congregation. If the congregation is deaf, the preacher will shout. If the congregation is slow, the preacher will not feed them too quickly. If the congregation is lazy, the preacher's job is to move them emotionally. The preacher needs to study the congregation to bring the Word of God to them at their level, and will, in this way, express God's compassion, patience and accommodation to their weakness. What a challenge for the preacher!

Thirdly, the preacher will realize that we cannot receive the words of God unless God acts within us by his Holy Spirit. So he or she will plead for a right understanding of Scripture in preparation for the sermon, pray for the congregation as they hear it, and urge the congregation to pray to God and appreciate their dependence on him.

Calvin thus provides a comprehensive, challenging and practical theology of preaching. We now look at Calvin's practice of preaching, to see how he implemented his theology in the context of his ministry.

John Calvin's practice of preaching

It will be recalled that Calvin preached two sermons each Sunday, and one each day in alternate weeks.[53] Later in his ministry his sermons were taken down in shorthand, edited and published, and many are available to us today. Calvin's method of preaching was expository, preaching on two or three verses in each sermon. A book such as Micah or 2 Timothy would require about twenty-eight sermons, Ephesians taking forty-eight.[54] His sermons lasted about forty minutes. His Sunday sermons were on the New Testament, his weekday sermons (at 6 or 7 am) on the Old Testament.

It is interesting to compare Calvin's preaching style with his writing style in the *Institutes* and the commentaries. It is especially important for those who try to follow the style of the *Institutes* in a pulpit ministry! Calvin wrote the *Institutes* to provide a summary of major doctrines, so that his commentaries could be shorter and less repetitive than they might otherwise have been. His idea was that if people read the *Institutes* first, they would then be able to read the commentaries with some theological background.[55] But all this is preparation, not the final product: the aim of the preparation is to help the preacher. The sermon is the final product, and in the sermon, as we have seen, the truths of God come home to the hearers through the ministry of the preacher.

For our first example of Calvin's preaching we take his sermon on one of the Ten Commandments, and begin by comparing it with his treatment of it in the *Institutes*. The commandment is, 'You shall not kill.'

In the *Institutes*, Calvin deals with the sixth commandment in two theologically dense paragraphs.[56] In the first, he makes the point that God has bound mankind together by a certain unity and hence we should be concerned for the safety of all. Therefore all violence and injury, and any harmful thing at all that may injure our neighbour's body, are forbidden to us. God the lawgiver is concerned not only with the body but with the soul as well; therefore this law also 'forbids murder of the heart, and enjoins the inner intent to save a brother's life'. In the second paragraph Calvin gives the theological reasons for the commandment which are found elsewhere in Scripture, namely that man is both the image of God and our flesh. He concludes with the reminder that if 'there is so much concern for the safety of his body, from this we may infer how much zeal and effort we owe the safety of the soul, which far excels the body in the Lord's sight'.[57]

The *sermon* on Deuteronomy 5:17 was preached on Monday 1 July 1555.[58] An interesting feature is that it offers an insight not only into Calvin's style of preaching and exhortation but also into current events in Geneva, including the Perrinist Tumult on 16 May 1555. The style is of continuous exhortation. It consists of thirty paragraphs, with the first twenty-one forming the main body. Paragraph 22 summarizes this, and then the final seven paragraphs give a series of applications.

Here are some representative paragraphs.

> . . . God spoke in a gross and uncultured manner in order to accommodate himself to the great and the small and the less intelligent. For we know that everyone excuses himself on the grounds of ignorance, and that if something appears too obscure and difficult, it seems to us that when we fail we can wash our hands of it if [only] we can say 'O that was too lofty and profound for me; I didn't understand it well at all.'

Therefore in order that men might no longer have [recourse] to such subterfuges, God willed to speak in such a way that little children can understand what he says. That is why, in sum, he says 'you shall not be murderers'. In addition, let us note that in order to lead us little to little toward upright living, God confronts us with the most detestable things in order that we might learn to guard against doing evil. For example, he could have easily said 'you shall not cause any injury to or violence against our neighbours'. He could have easily said that. But he wanted to emphasise murder. And why? [Because] it is a thing against nature for men to confront each other in such a way as to efface the image of God. Thus we hold murders in horror, unless we are stupid.[59]

Notice how Calvin explains the implications of God's accommodation to his hearers.

Now, nevertheless, seeing that God deals rather curtly with these things according to our ignorance and weakness let us note that it isn't enough not to spill blood; we must abstain from all outrage[ous acts] and violence. In brief men must be dear and precious to us. For until we arrive at that, God will always consider us murderers. If anyone strikes his neighbour, even though he does not kill him, he is still a murderer in God's sight. And why? We have already said that God expressly used this word in order to explain to us, that although people may consider quarrelling and street-fighting to be of a petty and inconsequential nature, God hardly considers it so. Why? Because murder is still involved. That is why God spoke the way he did.[60]

Again, Calvin is applying the message of the commandment clearly to his audience. His mention of street-fighting refers to the Perrinist revolt of several weeks earlier. Throughout, Calvin is trying to clarify the message of the Bible for his hearers.

In fact, that is the precise reason why St. John says that whoever hates his brother in his heart is [already] a murderer. It's as if he were saying: "Put on all the airs you want to even though your hate may be hidden and you hide your eyes against it, even if you don't show the slightest sign of ill will, don't think that God consequently has his eyes closed too." Men may never detect what you keep disclosed but when you hate your fellow man in your hearts, that is to say secretly, in such a way that no one can perceive it, indeed you are murderers in God's sight.[61]

Calvin's application of the commandment is to the common life of the people at Geneva and the way in which they express murder in their hearts.

> Besides, it we find it strange that God equates a slap in the face with murder, or for that matter a verbal insult, or sulking, that even though our lips may not have parted [he] still [condemns] our secret and hidden hate . . . if we find it strange that that should be equated with murder in God's sight, let us remember his nature and that he is indeed worthy of our attributing to him more than [we do] to earthly men. Now if earthly magistrates punish an evil deed when it is finally exposed, what will God do, to whom nothing is hidden?[62]

Calvin is also concerned to bring out the positive message of the commandment.

> Nevertheless, it is still necessary for us to go further than that. For is it not enough for men to abstain from doing evil, for they are created for the purpose of helping each other and supporting each other together. Therefore God, in forbidding us to murder, shows us the opposite, that we must hold our neighbour's life dear, that we must go to the trouble of both maintaining and preserving it as long as we possibly can.[63]

Calvin ends his sermon with an extended application.

> Now it remains for each [of us] to consider what we can do. When I have the means for helping my fellow-man, it is essential that I conclude that what God has given me is not mine . . . but when I have the means of supporting those who need my aid, I must engage myself to that end.[64]

> There is now a matter for the faithful to consider that far transcends this, for not only must they acknowledge that they are formed in the image of God, but they must also remember that they are members of our Lord Jesus Christ and that there exists [now] a more strict and sacred bond than the bond of nature which is common in all human beings . . . Therefore let us learn how to submit ourselves truly to what is said here, that being purged of all rancour and ill will, we might be advised to engage ourselves in the service of our fellow man and fulfill our obligation according to the means that God has given us.[65]

> Inasmuch as he is spirit he also wishes for us to worship him in such integrity that not only should our feet and hands be restrained but our hearts should be submissive to him.[66]

Calvin's concern is to show the relevance of the commandment to the everyday life of the citizens of Geneva.

This sermon is a fine example of preaching that is theologically weighty and pastorally appropriate. Calvin is true to his text in the theological context of the whole Bible, and he is true to his people in explaining and applying the text to their everyday lives.

For another example we compare Calvin's commentary on Ephesians 2:8–10 with his sermon on the same topic.

In his *commentary* on this passage he has eleven paragraphs to explain the text. Six of these consist of criticism of either the papists or the Pelagians. Even in his commentary Calvin writes of Paul speaking to us. His primary concern is not what Paul is saying to the Ephesians but what we have to learn from Paul's words in the letter.

In his *sermon* on the same passage he again has thirty paragraphs (his normal sermon length), and his language is again addressed to us and our pride. Interestingly, his method is to make continual application through every paragraph. He characteristically begins a paragraph with a theological discussion and ends it with a text which demonstrates what he has been saying.

> Here, therefore, he concludes that matter, and shows what he meant when he told us that our adoption hangs on and proceeds from God's choosing of us in his own everlasting purpose, that is to say, in order that we should be, as it were, bowed down to the dust, confessing that whatever we are and whatever goodness we have, we hold it wholly from God and of his free grace. That is the reason why he says 'we are saved by grace; not of ourselves, but by God's gift, and not by works'.[67]

Calvin uses vivid images to bring his message home. We are those who are 'as it were stark naked', we are 'rotten carcasses' and 'poor hungry souls', and those who are proud are 'swollen like toads'.[68] He uses questions to involve his audience:

> Well, you say, we will bring our good works as Papists are accustomed to do. How now? they argue. Shall we not be saved by our own merits and our own good works? And where do you get them from? says St. Paul. Have you coined them in your own shop, or have you some garden planted by yourself in which to gather them, or do they spring, I do not know how,

from your own labours and skill so that you may advance yourselves by them? No, for on the contrary, you know that God has prepared them. And is it fitting that you should go about raising objections against him when he has pitied you and showed himself bountiful towards you? Is it becoming that you should presume to step forward to pay him, and say that you have money of your own?[69]

This last question introduces Calvin's image of a man who has been well kept and looked after by his host, and then given money by his host to pay for his board and lodging.

Calvin spends four of his thirty paragraphs attacking the ideas of the papists. There are three comments to make on this. First, the papists provide a kind of theological foil for the clarity of Calvin's Reformation doctrine. Secondly, the citizens of Geneva had been raised as papists and Calvin was still attempting to rid Geneva of these theological ideas. Thirdly, it may be that attacking papists was Calvin's conventional way of padding out a sermon.

In our final example of Calvin's preaching, we notice how much the strength of Calvin's sermons derives from the pastoral ministry, as again and again he verbalizes the instinctive responses of his people to the message of the Bible, and answers these objections by returning again to his text. In his sermon Calvin creates a vivid and realistic dialogue between the text and his people.

This sermon is Calvin's thirty-ninth on Ephesians,[70] which was meant to be on 5:22–26, though he only gets as far as verse 25. It has thirty-one paragraphs, of which I give a prècis by taking one sentence from each paragraph.

We have seen so far how each one of us is subject to his neighbours, and that we cannot live otherwise one with another, other than by engaging in some duty and token of subjection. However, when God has joined people together by a closer and holier tie, every man must look more closely to himself. You see then that what we have to deal with now is that we are to live in love with one another, endeavouring to discharge the duty God places upon us, according to our ability. And now let us come to marriage which is not a thing ordained by men: we know that God is the author of it, and that it is solemnised in his name. Now then, if a wife be cross-grained, and cannot find in her heart to bear the yoke, although she does wrong to her husband, yet God is still more outraged. On the other hand when a man will insist on lording it after his own liking and fancy, despising his wife, or use her cruelly or tyrannically, he shows that he despises God and defies him openly. For he ought to know for what purpose he was created, what the state of marriage is, and what law God has set in it.

The husband may plead 'I have a dreadful and stubborn wife' or else 'she is proud or has a wicked head' or is else 'too talkative'. The wife also for her part will not be without stock of excuses. For often her husband may be irritable or quarrelsome, with little regard to what God has called them to. Some are niggardly and frequentous of taverns, or else act like spendthrifts in gaming and other dissolute practices, some whoremongers, some gluttons, and some drunkards. And so every woman might pretend some excuse to exempt herself from her duty. But when we come to God, we are bound to hang down our heads for it will profit us nothing to be insolent towards him. Therefore let us learn to note well St. Paul's doctrine, that just as marriage was ordained by God, so they that are to enter into it must turn wholly to him and make him their refuge, knowing that it is God who binds the man and the wife the one to the other, and who joined them together. Therefore each of them must pay heed to their respective duties.

Rather did he join the man and the woman together in such a way, that the man knowing his wife to be as his own substance and flesh should be induced thereby to love her, that the wife, knowing herself to have no other being but of the man, should bear her subjection patiently and with a voluntary affection. For if the hand, being a member of the body, should refuse to stay in its own place and should insist upon settling itself upon the crown of the head, what a thing it would be!

For it is certain that if Eve and Adam had continued in the righteousness that God had given them, the whole state of this terrestrial life would have been like paradise, and marriage would have been so ordered that husband and wife being joined together should have lived in such harmony as we see the angels in paradise do. Therefore when now a man has a harsh and dreadful wife, whom he cannot manage by any means, let him know, Here are the fruits of original sin and also of the corruption that is in myself. And the wife also on her side must think, 'There is good reason that I should receive the payment that comes from my disobedience towards God, because I did not humble myself before him.'

Therefore let us know that St. Paul has not used this similitude to join husbands (who are mortal creatures and no more than poor worms of the earth) in equal rank with Jesus

Christ, but to show briefly that since our Lord Jesus presides over marriage men must have an eye to him, and every person submit himself patiently. And also let the husbands think on their duty . . . they should not be cruel towards their wives, or think all things that they please to be permissible and lawful, for their authority ought rather be a companionship than a kingship. For there is no question that a husband is not his wife's head to oppress her or to make no account of her.

But most commonly it is to be seen that men deal roughly with their wives, and think of winning them by dreadful behaviour so that they do not hesitate to bruise their bodies and sometimes to cause the blood to flow. These are hangmen that will thus make the lives of their wives a hell and yet they will plead the superiority that God gives them. And now the women on their side harden themselves for the most part . . . they plot among themselves saying 'Oh, I warrant I will hold my own, and if my husband behaves dreadfully to me, I will show him that I do not care what he does. After I have held out against him for a few days he will find that he is wasting his time, and then he will have to give up his game and leave me alone.'

Now St. Paul puts forward our Lord Jesus Christ to the husbands also in order that they should not abuse the authority that is granted them, nor break the friendship that ought to be maintained in marriage by being too cruel, as they are accustomed to be. Rather men should think 'He will have me to behave myself towards my wife as Jesus Christ has behaved himself towards me'. Is not this enough to break hearts that were hard as stone? Yea as steel? Yes surely. Likewise if the women on their side are mindful of their redemption and salvation, then their hard hearts will be softened. They would not harden themselves any more to such stubbornness as they do, but would submit themselves to the yoke of our Lord Jesus Christ that they might be partakers of the benefit he has purchased for them by his death and passion.

Now then, on the one hand let the husbands consider well here what they owe to their wives, that is to say, that they should be as dear to them as their own lives at least . . . and the wives also for their part must bear well in mind that since it is God's will that in wedlock they should be, as it were, a type of the grace of our Lord Jesus Christ, they are much too ungrateful if they do not submit themselves where God calls them to it. If we keep these things in mind, on the one hand we shall be moved to our duty without disputing. Then too we shall be set afire to glorify our God and acknowledge both with our mouths and also by our whole life how much we are indebted to him, seeing that he has poured out the treasures of his mercy upon us.

What comments can we make about Calvin's preaching?

First, it is important to keep in mind Calvin's doctrine of God's accommodation to us, not only to humankind in general but also to a particular congregation. God's accommodation means that he provides the congregation not only with the Bible but also with the preacher who will accommodate the message of the Bible to its members' needs and apply it directly to them. Therefore Calvin's style and manner of preaching may not be appropriate for another congregation. He clearly distinguishes between his commentaries and *Institutes*, which are of universal significance, and his sermons, which are of particular relevance to his own congregation. It would be a great mistake for us to repeat Calvin's style, manner or content of preaching in our own congregations.

Secondly, Calvin has such a strong sense that the Bible is God speaking to us that he often fails to distinguish between the original and the present audience. To put it another way, he treats the Bible as God's Word directly to us without taking good account of its historical context. Perhaps Calvin is more likely to make this mistake in the epistles of the New Testament which are more easily applied directly to us. Certainly in his Old Testament sermons he is more aware of the gap between the original and the present audience. For example, in his sermons on 2 Samuel[71] he clearly distinguishes between the text and what he calls 'gathering the fruit from it'.[72]

Thirdly, Calvin's style of application is to use 'we' and 'us' rather than 'you'. It may well be that this style was suitable for his congregation. I suspect that it is appropriate for us nowadays to use a mixture of 'us' and 'we' language and 'you' language. The 'us' and 'we' language makes the point that the Bible's message is to preacher and congregation alike, that we all stand under God's judgment and mercy and are all addressed by the words of God through the Bible. The 'you' language makes it clear that the preacher is speaking on behalf of God and addressing the congregation with the words of God.

Fourthly, Calvin's sermons have a common length; he used to preach for forty minutes.[73] Presumably this fitted in with Calvin's belief about the ability of the congregation to hear, and is not a statutory requirement for all preachers and all congregations.

Fifthly, Calvin's language of appeal is restrained. When he talks about preaching and the job of a preacher, he uses language of extravagance and seems to commend a strong appeal to the congregation, but in his own preaching it is not easy to detect a high emotional tone. Perhaps again this was Calvin's accommodation to the mixed congregation to whom he preached.

Our subject in this chapter has been the purpose of preaching. I have argued that as preachers we should be serving God and Christ, serving the Word of God, and serving the people of God. Calvin demonstrated this priority of servanthood, of ministry, in both his theology and his practice of preaching. His theology of God's accommodating his speaking to us in Scripture, in the preachers he sends and by His Holy Spirit, provides us with a robust, positive and challenging theology of the preacher's task. In a few examples of Calvin's own preaching we saw how he put into practice his own theology of preaching, and accommodated himself with integrity, understanding and compassion to his own congregation.

Notes

1. Charles Simeon, *Expository Outlines on the Whole Bible* (reprint of the 8th edn of *Horae Homiliticae*, 1847); Grand Rapids: Baker, 1988), vol. 1, p. xxi. Note the individualistic emphasis!

2. Stott, *The Contemporary Christian*, p. 208.

3. For more on expository preaching, see Parker, *Calvin's Preaching*, ch. 9; Robinson, *Expository Preaching*; John MacArthur Jr, *Rediscovering Expository Preaching* (Waco: Word, 1992). For lessons in expository preaching, I can think of no better source than the sermons of John Chrysostom and John Calvin.

4. Thomas K. Carroll, *Preaching the Word: The Message of the Fathers of the Church* (Wilmington: Michael Glazier, 1984), pp. 63, 197, 206, 220.

5. Klaas Runia, *The Sermon under Attack* (Exeter: Paternoster, 1983), p. 63.

6. *Ibid.*, p. 71.

7. Brueggemann, *Finally Comes the Poet*, ch. 2.

8. Quoted from Calvin's forty-nine sermons on Job by Runia, *The Sermon under Attack*, p. 74.

9. Highly recommended are 'Puritan Preaching', in Packer, *A Quest for Godliness = Among God's Giants*, and John Piper, *The Supremacy of God in Preaching* (Grand Rapids: Baker; Leicester: IVP, 1990), mainly on the preaching of Jonathan Edwards.

10. Packer, *A Quest for Godliness = Among God's Giants*, p. 379.

11. William Perkins, *An Instruction Touching Religious or Divine Worship*, in Ian Breward (ed.), *William Perkins* (Abingdon: Sutton Courtenay Press, 1970), p. 315.

12. *Ibid.*, p. 333.

13. *Ibid.*, p. 340.

14. *Ibid.*, p. 341.

15. *Ibid.*, p. 342.

16. Augustine, *On Catechising* (Eng. trans. Edinburgh: T. and T. Clark, 3rd edn, 1883), pp. 300–301.

17. *The Directory for the Public Worship of God* (London: Wickliffe Press, 1958), p. 380.

18. I am greatly indebted for this section to T. H. L. Parker, *The Oracles of God* (London: Lutterworth, 1947); *idem*, *Calvin's Preaching*; Ronald S. Wallace, *Calvin's Doctrine of the Word and Sacrament* (Edinburgh: Oliver and Boyd,

1953); and W. de Greef, *The Writings of John Calvin: An Introductory Guide* (Eng. trans. Grand Rapids: Baker; Leicester: Apollos, 1993).

19. See especially Ford L. Battles, 'God was Accommodating himself to Human Capacity', in *Interpretation* 31 (January 1977), pp. 21–47.

20. Commentary on 1 Peter 1:20, quoted in *ibid.*, p. 38.

21. J. I. Packer, 'Calvin the Theologian', in *John Calvin* (Abingdon: Sutton Courtenay Press, 1966), p. 162.

22. Calvin, *Institutes*, I.xiii.1, p. 121.

23. *Ibid.*, I.xi.1, pp. 99–100.

24. Calvin, *Sermons on the Ten Commandments*, ed. and trans. Benjamin Farley (Grand Rapids: Baker, 1980), p. 153.

25. *Commentary on John* (3:12) in Calvin's *Commentaries*, Library of Christian Classics 23, ed. Joseph Haroutunian (London: SCM, 1958), p. 90.

26. Calvin, *Institutes* IV. iii. 1, p. 1053.

27. *Ibid.*, IV.i.5, p. 1018.

28. *Ibid.*, IV.iii.1, p. 1053.

29. *Ibid.*, IV.iii.1, p. 1054.

30. *Ibid.*

31. *Ibid.*, IV.i.5, pp. 1017–1018.

32. *Ibid.*

33. Calvin, *Sermons on the Epistle to the Ephesians* (on 4:11–14) (Eng. trans. Edinburgh: Banner of Truth, 1973), p. 376.

34. Calvin, *Commentary on a Harmony of the Gospels*, quoted in Graham Miller, *Calvin's Wisdom* (Edinburgh: Banner of Truth, 1992), p. 255.

35. Calvin, *Commentary on the Four Last Books of Moses*, quoted in *ibid.*, p. 253.

36. Calvin, *Sermons on Timothy and Titus* (Eng. trans. 1579; facsimile reprint Edinburgh: Banner of Truth, 1983), p. 945. Quotations from this volume are slightly modified.

37. *Ibid.*, p. 947.

38. *Ibid.*, p. 1199.

39. *Ibid.*, p. 1200.

40. *Ibid.*, p. 419.

41. Quoted in the Publishers' Introduction to Calvin, *Sermons on Ephesians*, p. x.

42. Calvin, *Commentary on 1 Corinthians* (on 12:28) (Eng. trans. Grand Rapids: Eerdmans, 1960), p. 271.

43. Calvin, *Commentary on Isaiah* (on 1:30), quoted in Miller, *Calvin's Wisdom*, pp. 253–254.

44. Quoted in Calvin, *Sermons on the Ten Commandments*, p. 29.

45. Calvin, sermon on 2 Timothy 1:2, quoted in Parker, *Calvin's Preaching*, p. 42.

46. Calvin, *Commentary on Ephesians*, quoted in *ibid.* p. 42.

47. Calvin, *Institutes* I.ix.3, p. 95.

48. *Ibid.*, II.v.5, p. 322.

49. Calvin, comment on John 14:26, *Commentary on John*, p. 397.

50. Calvin, comment on John 16:8, *ibid.*, p. 399.

51. Calvin, comment on 1 Timothy 3:9, quoted in Parker, *Calvin's Preaching*, p. 51.

52. Calvin, *Sermons on Ephesians* (on 2:8–10), p. 161.

53. Parker, *Calvin's Preaching*, chapter 7. See above, pp. 62–63.

54. *Ibid.*, ch. 9.

55. Parker, 'Calvin the Biblical Expositor', pp. 182–183. See especially n. 17.

56. Calvin, *Institutes* II.viii.39–40, pp. 404–405.

57. *Ibid.*, II.viii.40, p. 405.

58. Calvin, *Sermons on the Ten Commandments*, pp. 151ff.

59. *Ibid.*, p. 153.

60. *Ibid.*, pp. 156–157.

61. *Ibid.*, p. 159.

62. *Ibid.*, pp. 160–161.

63. *Ibid.*, p. 161.

64. *Ibid.*, p. 164–165.

65. *Ibid.*, p. 165.

66. *Ibid.*, p. 166.

67. Calvin, *Sermons on Ephesians*, p. 155.

68. *Ibid.*, pp. 156–160.

69. *Ibid.*, p. 165.

70. *Ibid.*, pp. 564–576.

71. Calvin, *Sermons on 2 Samuel* (Eng. trans. Edinburgh: Banner of Truth, 1992).

72. *Ibid.*, pp. 431, 434.

73. Publishers' Introduction to Calvin, *Sermons on Ephesians*, p. xv, n. 1.

7

The demands of preaching

In Part 1 we studied the three great theological foundations of preaching: *God has spoken*, *It is written*, and *Preach the word*. In Part 2 we have been investigating the work of the preacher. In chapter 4 we looked at preaching as a ministry of the Word, and at its special and crucial role as 'the explanation and application of the Word to the congregation of Christ, in order to produce corporate preparation for service, unity of faith, maturity, growth and upbuilding'. In chapter 5 we studied the preacher's Bible, and the ways in which the nature and theology of the Bible should inform our preaching. In chapter 6 we studied the preacher's purpose (to serve God and Christ, to serve the Word of God, and to serve the people of God), and we discovered how Calvin's theology and practice of preaching exemplified these aims. In this final chapter we look at the demands of preaching.

In his book *I Believe in Preaching* John Stott quotes the following image of the preacher.

> Although in the rather flowery language of a century ago, Matthew Simpson gave an admirable summary of the unique-ness of the sermon event. He wrote of the preacher: 'His throne is the pulpit; he stands in Christ's stead; his message is the word of God; around him are immortal souls; the Saviour, unseen, is beside him; the Holy Spirit broods over the congregation; angels gaze upon the scene, and heaven and hell await the issue. What associations, and what vast responsibil-ity!'[1]

There is no better place to see the demanding nature of the preaching ministry than in Paul's description of his own ministry in 1 and 2 Corinthians. He describes it as ministry of the new covenant (2 Cor. 3:6), and this is a ministry shared by all ministers of the Word. We shall examine Paul's picture of the life of new-covenant ministry under seven headings: love and obedience to God and Christ; commitment to the truth of God; love for people; hard work and time; relating to the real world in which people live; suffering; and the assurance that our sufficiency is from God.

Love and obedience to God and Christ

It may seem superfluous to mention that preaching is a ministry which involves love and obedience to God and Christ. A ministry which is so central in God's mind and to God's plan must surely have the honour and glory of God and of Christ as its chief aim. Sadly this is not necessarily the case; it is very easy to engage in any form of ministry, including that of preaching, for many reasons other than love for and obedience to God and Christ. We may become people-centred in our ministry so that our main aim becomes helping them; or our aim may be to perform our ministry well, to preach well, to preach effectively. These are good aims, but they focus on the means rather than the end, and if they stand by themselves they become a form of idolatry; we either serve other people in place of God or we serve our own ego in place of God. It is particularly important for the preacher to know that he is answerable to God. The fact is that our primary responsibility is to be servants of God and of Christ. The moment we take our eyes off the service of God to serve others or to serve ourselves, our ministry suffers. This also means that our ministry cannot be evaluated in this life, but we must wait until the return of Christ to understand fully what God has done through us, and for our ministry to be evaluated. We should avoid the impulsive tendency to gauge our progress, to estimate our success or our failure by merely human means.

Our faith must be in the God who not only works generally in the world, but has also called us to ministry and has promised to work in the particular sermon that we are now preparing or preaching. John Owen[2] refers to three spiritual gifts which are necessary for the teaching ministry. The first is wisdom or knowledge or understanding.

> Such a comprehension of the scope of the Scripture and of the revelation of God therein; such an acquaintance with the systems of particular doctrinal truths, in their rise, tendency, and use; such a habit in mind of judging spiritual things, and comparing them one with another; such a distinct insight into the springs and course of the mystery of the love, grace and will of God in Christ as enables them in whom it is to declare the counsel of God, to make known the way of life, of faith and obedience unto others, and to instruct them in their whole duty to God and man therein.[3]

The second gift is 'skill to divide the Word aright which is also a peculiar gift of the Holy Ghost'.[4] One of the most valuable elements in

Puritan teaching about ministry is the constant stress laid on the need for discerning and discriminating application. Owen sets out in detail what is required for the use of this gift.

> Sound judgement in general concerning the state and condition of those unto whom anyone is so dispensing the Word. It is the duty of a shepherd to know the state of his flock; and unless he do so he will never feed them profitably. He must know whether they are babes or young men or old, whether they need milk or strong meat . . . whether in judgement of charity they are converted unto God, or are yet in an unregenerate condition. What probably are their principal temptations, their hindrances and furtherances, what is their growth or decay?
>
> An acquaintance with the ways and methods of the work of God's grace on the minds and hearts of men that he may pursue and comply with its design of a ministry of the Word . . . he . . . who is unacquainted with the ordinary methods of the operation of grace fights uncertainly in his preaching of the Word like a man beating of the air. It is true God can and often doth direct a word of truth spoken as it were at random unto a proper effect of grace on some or other . . . but ordinarily a man is not likely to hit a joint [target] who knows not how to take his aim.
>
> An acquaintance with the nature of temptation . . . many things might be added on this head . . . for a right understanding of the nature of spiritual diseases, distempers and sicknesses with their proper cures and remedies belonging there unto. For the want hereof the hearts of the wicked are oftentimes made glad in the preaching of the Word and those of the righteous filled with sorrow. The hands of sinners are strengthened and those who are looking towards God are discouraged or turned out of the way.[5]

Thirdly, with knowledge of God's truth and skill to apply must go the gift of utterance which, says Owen, is particularly reckoned by the apostle among the gifts of the Spirit. It consists of naturalness appropriate to the subject matter, plus boldness and holy confidence, plus gravity 'and that authority which accompanieth the delivery of the Word when preached in demonstration of these spiritual abilities. All these things are necessary . . . that the hearers may receive the Word not as the word of man but as it is indeed the Word of God'.[6]

Owen warns that 'a ministry devoid of spiritual gifts is sufficient evidence of a church under a degenerating apostasy'.[7] Faith in the present work of God who has called us to be preachers of the Word is important, otherwise we may continue preaching out of sheer obedience but without confidence, without joy and without hope. It is a sure sign that we are in fact believing in preaching rather than in God.

To believe in God is to believe in the work of his Holy Spirit. John Stott describes how C. H. Spurgeon walked up the steps of the massive central pulpit at the Metropolitan Tabernacle, saying as he mounted each step, 'I believe in the Holy Ghost.' Stott quotes Spurgeon:

> The gospel is preached in the ears of all; it only comes with power to some. The power that is in the gospel does not lie in the eloquence of the preacher; otherwise men would be the converters of souls. Nor does it lie in the preacher's learning; otherwise it would consist in the wisdom of men. We might preach till our tongues rotted, till we should exhaust our lungs and die, but never a soul would be converted unless there were a mysterious power going with it – the Holy Ghost changing the will of man. Oh Sirs! We might as well preach to stone walls as preach to humanity unless the Holy Ghost be with the word, to give it power to convert the soul.[8]

All this means that it ought to be clearly evident to those to whom we minister that our primary duty and loyalty are to God and Christ. We may then say, 'We are your servants, but you are not our rulers: God alone is our ruler and judge.'

Commitment to the truth of God

This love and obedience to God and to Christ require faithfulness to the truth that has been revealed by God. 'We speak God's wisdom, secret and hidden, which God decreed before the ages for our glory' (1 Cor. 2:7). Paul sees himself not as an innovator but rather as a servant of God, passing on the message that he has received. 'For I handed on to you as of first importance what I in turn had received: that Christ died for our sins in accordance with the scriptures, and that he was buried, that he was raised on the third day in accordance with the scriptures, and that he appeared to Cephas, then to the twelve' (1 Cor. 15:3–5).

Paul asserts the truth not only because people need to learn it and to be reminded of it, but also because his opponents are promoting falsehoods and because Satan's design is to draw people away from the Lord Jesus Christ. 'But I am afraid that just as the serpent deceived Eve by its cunning your thoughts will be led astray from a sincere and pure devotion to Christ' (2 Cor. 11:3). As Calvin says, 'To assert the truth is only one half of the office of preaching . . . except all the fallacies of the devil be also dissipated.'[9]

John MacArthur Jr pictures the cost of being a servant of the Word of God, of searching for the truth, in these striking words:

> Fling him into his office. Tear the 'Office' sign from the door and nail on the sign, 'Study'. Take him off the mailing list. Lock him up with his books and his typewriter and his Bible. Slam him down on his knees before texts and broken hearts and the lives of a superficial flock and a holy God.
>
> Force him to be the one man in our surfeited communities who knows about God. Throw him into the ring to box with God until he learns how short his arms are. Engage him to wrestle with God all the night through. And let him come out only when he's bruised and beaten into being a blessing.
>
> Shut his mouth forever spouting remarks, and stop his tongue forever tripping lightly over every non-essential. Require him to have something to say before he dares break the silence. Bend his knees in the lonesome valley.
>
> Burn his eyes with weary study. Wreck his emotional poise with worry for God. And make him exchange his pious stance for a humble walk with God and man. Make him spend and be spent for the glory of God. Rip out his telephone. Burn up his ecclesiastical success sheets.
>
> Put water in his gas [petrol] tank. Give him a Bible and tie him to the pulpit. And make him preach the Word of the living God!
>
> Test him. Quiz him. Examine him. Humiliate him for his ignorance of things divine. Shame him for his good comprehension of finances, batting averages, and political in-fighting. Laugh at his frustrated effort to play psychiatrist. Form a choir and raise a chant and haunt him with it night and day – 'Sir, we would see Jesus.'
>
> When at long last he dares assay the pulpit, ask him if he has a word from God. If he does not, then dismiss him. Tell him you can read the morning paper and digest the television commentaries, and think through the day's superficial problems, and manage the community's weary drives, and bless the sordid baked potatoes and green beans, *ad infinitum*, better than he can.
>
> Command him not to come back until he's read and reread, written and rewritten, until he can stand up, worn and forlorn, and say, 'Thus saith the Lord.'
>
> Break him across the board of his ill-gotten popularity. Smack him hard with his own prestige. Corner him with questions about God. Cover him with demands for celestial

wisdom. And give him no escape until he's back against the wall of the Word.

And sit down before him and listen to the only word he has left – God's Word. Let him be totally ignorant of the down-street gossip, but give him a chapter and order him to walk around it, camp on it, sup with it, and come at last to speak it backward and forward, until all he says about it rings with the truth of eternity.

And when he's burned out by the flaming Word, when he's consumed at last by the fiery grace blazing through him, and when he's privileged to translate the truth of God to man, finally transferred from earth to heaven, then bear him away gently and blow a muted trumpet and lay him down softly. Place a two-edged sword in his coffin, and raise the tomb triumphant. For he was a brave soldier of the Word. And ere he died, he had become a man of God.[10]

Great stuff – but the preacher needs to know the congregation as well! And the teaching elder will have wider responsibilities than preparing sermons!

Love for people

We must recognize in Paul's ministry of preaching the great love for people which he is not ashamed to express. He describes his previous letter to the Corinthians in these terms: 'I wrote to you out of much distress and anguish of heart and with many tears, not to cause you pain, but to let you know the abundant love that I have for you' (2 Cor. 2:4). 'I will most gladly spend and be spent for you. If I love you more, am I to be loved less?' (2 Cor. 12:15). 'My love be with you all in Christ Jesus' (1 Cor. 16:24). Paul's love for the Corinthians is reflected in the care, thoughtfulness and compassion of his ministry among them. 'I fed you with milk, not solid food, for you were not ready for solid food' (1 Cor. 3:2). 'We write to you nothing other than what you can read and also understand' (2 Cor. 1:13). It is because of his great love and concern for everyone that he has given up his rights as an apostle. 'Though I am free with respect to all, I have made myself a slave to all, so that I might win more of them . . . I have become all things to all people, so that I might by any means save some' (1 Cor. 9:19, 22).

For Paul, this love for all people and especially for his friends at Corinth is only a particular instance of that love which is required of all who engage in Christian ministry.

If I speak in the tongues of mortals and of angels, but do not have love, I am a noisy gong or a clanging cymbal. And if I have

> prophetic powers, and understand all mysteries and all know-
> ledge, and if I have all faith, so as to remove mountains, but do
> not have love, I am nothing. If I give away all my possessions,
> and if I hand over my body so that I may boast, but do not have
> love, I gain nothing.
>
> Love is patient; love is kind; love is not envious or boastful or
> arrogant or rude. It does not insist on its own way; it is not
> irritable or resentful; it does not rejoice in wrongdoing, but
> rejoices in the truth. It bears all things, believes all things,
> hopes all thing, endures all things. (1 Cor. 13:1–7)

Here Paul contrasts his own pattern of ministry with the self-centred,
destructive ministry of the false teachers at Corinth. Paul's ministry is
based on the truth of God and on a self-giving love for the Corinthians, a
ministry which edifies.

We all know that this love for people ought to underlie our ministry.
But those of us engaged in ministry know that this is often very far from
the case. It is a particular issue for those engaged in preaching ministry.
For there are very many different models of parish ministry available
today. My observation is that those who like people tend to go in for
counselling, small-group work, training and discipleship, in which they
are engaging with people constantly. Those who really do not like people
tend to go in for administration – or preaching!

To be servants of the Word it is not enough to love preaching: we have
to love people. To love preaching means that we are loving our own
actions, that we enjoy the ministry we do. To call it a ministry is a
deception, because we are not ministering or serving anyone but ourselves
and our sense of achievement. To love effective ministry is not enough, to
love success in ministry is not enough, to love achievement in ministry is
not enough. We must love people as well. Our ministry is a means to an
end, and its only value lies in the extent to which it serves the people who
hear us. Why else would we call it a ministry? As John Killinger puts it,
'The preacher's first calling therefore is to love. It is not enough to be in
love with preaching, it is not even enough to be in love with God.'[11]

It is one of the curious features of those who take preaching seriously
that they often love books rather than people. John Stott quotes David
Reid's 'ideal building plan for church and manse'. 'The salient feature was
a long straight corridor with a door at one end leading out of the manse
study and a door at the other end opening into the pulpit of the church
. . . the highway for the Word of the Lord, the straight path from the
mind of the preacher to the hearts of his hearers.'[12] Martyn Lloyd-Jones
quotes Richard Cecil, an Anglican preacher in London at the end of the
eighteenth century: 'To love to preach is one thing, to love those to whom
we preach quite another.'[13] To quote Charles Simeon: 'Let your preaching

come from your heart. Love should be the spring of all actions, and especially of a Minister's. If a man's heart be full of love, he will rarely offend.'[14] A good test of love of people for those who like books is this: when you buy the next book, is it because you would love to have the book, or because you love your people and want to use this book to help in your preparation to serve them? When you pray for your preaching, do you pray that you will preach well, or that the people will hear and receive your ministry and that it will bear fruit in your lives? Are you praying for yourself or for your people? Are you praying for your own achievement or for their edification?

We often make the mistake of thinking that if we do not love our people we can cover this effectively by a show of concern and compassion; but, as Leander Keck says: 'Just as preaching love without truth becomes chatter, so preaching the truth without love becomes a shrill voice of alienation. Whoever wants to preach prophetically must earn the moral right to do so by compassionate critical solidarity with those addressed. It is not enough to be right.'[15]

Our love for the people to whom we preach will be particularly evident by the care with which we not only open up the passage and give them the truth, but also by the care with which we apply the truth personally and appropriately to their lives.

The Westminster *Directory for the Public Worship of God* gives the following instruction to the preacher, highlighting the practical results of a loving ministry:

> He is not to rest in general doctrine, although never so much cleared and confirmed, but to bring it home to special use, by application to his hearers: which albeit prove a great work of difficulty to himself, requiring much prudence, zeal, and meditation, and to the natural and corrupt man will be very unpleasant; yet he is to endeavour to perform it in such a manner that his auditors may feel the Word of God to be quick and powerful and a discerner of the thoughts and intent of the heart . . . In exhorting to duties, he is, as he seeth cause to teach also the means that help to the performance of them. In dehortation, reprehension and public admonition (which require special wisdom) let him, as there shall be cause, not only discover the nature and greatness of the sin, with the misery attending it, but also show the danger his hearers are in to be overtaken and surprised by it, together with the remedies and best way to avoid it. In applying comfort, whether general against all temptations or particular against some special troubles or terrors, he is carefully to answer such objections as a troubled heart and afflicted spirit may suggest to the contrary.

And, as he needeth not always to prosecute every doctrine which lies in his text, so is he wisely to make choice of such uses, as by his residence and conversing with his flock, he findeth most needful and seasonable; and, amongst these, such as may most draw their souls to Christ the fountain of light, holiness and comfort.[16]

The servant of Christ, whatever his method be, is to perform his whole ministry:

1. Painfully, not doing the work of God negligently.

2. Plainly, that the meanest may understand . . .

3. Faithfully, looking at the honour of Christ, the conversion, edification and salvation of the people, not at his own gain or glory; keeping nothing back which may promote those holy ends, giving to everyone his own portion, and bearing indifferent respect unto all, without neglecting the meanest, or sparing the greatest, in their sins.

4. Wisely, framing all his doctrines, exhortations and especially his reproofs, in such a manner as may be most likely to prevail; showing all due respect to each person and place, and not mixing his own passion or bitterness.

5. Gravely, as becometh the Word of God; shunning all such gesture, voice, and expressions, as may occasion the corruptions of men to despise him and his ministry.

6. With loving affection, that the people may see all coming from his godly zeal and hearty desire to do them good.

7. As taught of God and persuaded in his own heart that all he teacheth is the truth of Christ . . .[17]

Hard work and time

Paul clearly understood his ministry to be hard work. He described it as 'the work of the Lord' and 'labour in the Lord' (1 Cor. 15:58). I think this means not only that Paul worked long hours in his ministry, but also that he understood that his ministry was intellectually and emotionally draining because he was absolutely committed to God and to the people in his care. It was intellectually demanding because he used his mind to grasp the truth of God, and to understand the theological issues raised by the state of his congregations and by the false teachers. It was emotionally demanding because he was emotionally committed to God and to his people and their welfare. 'I came to you in weakness and in fear and in much trembling. My speech and my proclamation were not with plausible words of wisdom, but with a demonstration of the Spirit and of power, so that your faith might rest not on human wisdom but on the power of God' (1 Cor. 2:3–5). 'If we are being afflicted, it is for your consolation and salvation; if we are being consoled, it is for your consolation, which you experience when you patiently endure the same sufferings that we are also suffering' (2 Cor. 1:6). 'I wrote to you out of much distress and anguish of heart and with many tears, not to cause you pain but to let you know the abundant love that I have for you' (2 Cor. 2:4). Have you told your congregation that you love them?

Because the ministry that Paul was engaged in was God's ministry, we might think that the apostle could be a merely passive agent. But this is not the case. It is precisely because God was working, and Paul was his fellow worker, that the apostle was called to a strenuous and demanding ministry. 'We are ambassadors for Christ, since God is making his appeal through us; we entreat you on behalf of Christ, be reconciled to God . . . As we work together with [God], we urge you also not to receive the grace of God in vain' (2 Cor. 5:20; 6:1). Paul's commitment to the Corinthians was not only a passionate commitment to them and to their welfare, but also a passionate concern for their obedience to Christ. For Paul this ministry was a matter of daily care. 'Besides other things, I am under daily pressure because of my anxiety for all the churches. Who is weak, and I am not weak? Who is made to stumble, and I am not indignant?' (2 Cor. 11:28–29).

It costs hard work *and time*. Ministers' lives are so full of administration, meetings, counselling and 'being available', that we find it hard to make time to prepare our sermons. As we have seen, we need double time for our sermons, so that we can work on both the text and the application. Charles Simeon usually spent twelve hours in the preparation of one sermon – and many took two or three days.[18] We show that we are rushed for time in our preparation when we have only a superficial understanding of the text, when we have no ideas on how to apply it, and when, as Browne puts it, 'unresolved conflicts in the preacher's mind show themselves by excessive speed over unmade roads in the course of the sermon's journey'.[19]

How will busy ministers find this sort of time? Here are some ideas.

Do not try and add this time to your present activities. Decide what you will cut out for twelve hours a week to prepare your sermon. Say no in order to say yes.

Educate your people about the importance of preaching (Calvin preached on 1 and 2 Timothy to do this), so that they will understand what you are doing.

Have one desk for administration and another for sermon preparation (I have different studies).

Allocate your preparation time over several days (*e.g.* four three-hour blocks), so that your subconscious mind can work on your sermon while you are doing something else.

Plan your preparation time weeks ahead, and keep to your timetable.

Show your people that you love them by the time you spend in prayer and preparation.

Relating to the real world

One of the fascinating features of 1 and 2 Corinthians is the clear way in which Paul is writing not general Christian instruction for anyone who wants to read, but instruction particularly addressed to the Corinthians. This is evident not only in that Paul is replying to a letter that they have written to him (1 Cor. 7:1), but also in that there is so much detailed instruction which demonstrates Paul's deep and loving knowledge of their context and world. This knowledge means that Paul is able to speak directly and appropriately to their condition, and is a sign of his love for them. 1 and 2 Corinthians are occasional letters in the sense that they are both written to address the serious issues of the Corinthian church at that time. The preacher must be similarly concerned to deal with the real world of the congregation individually and corporately. This means looking beyond the congregation as they present themselves on a Sunday in order to understand what is going on behind their church-attending façades. True preaching, though a monologue in form, will be a dialogue in content. 1 and 2 Corinthians are a continuous response to issues raised by the Corinthians or issues that Paul sees as important in their lives.

Our style of preaching means that the listeners are essentially passive and unable to object. They get accustomed to giving the appearance of passive and docile acceptance of what we say, though their hearts and minds may be very far away from the words we are saying. There are many factors which make it difficult for people to engage in the task of listening to sermons.[20] The communication patterns of our age do not make room for listening to sermons. If people's major way of receiving information is through television or a computer – through visual images – they will find it difficult to listen to sermons. It is also true that people have been conditioned by our society, since the Enlightenment, to be suspicious of any external authority and to distrust anything which they cannot see or prove for themselves. This makes it difficult for them to listen to sermons which claim some authority from God. Further, many people in our society echo the words of Henry Ford, 'History is bunk.' Preaching from a document which is 2,000 years old or more therefore erects a great barrier for our congregations. Again, our need to present a sermon within a certain length of time means that we are always summarizing, and in danger of trivializing, serious matters. Many of our congregation may feel that life is more complex than can be covered in a sermon of twenty to forty minutes. Finally, our congregations are aware that there is a great deal of controversy about the use of the Bible, its meaning, and whether indeed the Bible is worth studying.

I am not suggesting for a moment that we ought to give up preaching, but that in our preaching we ought to be deeply aware of issues people face and which are no doubt deep within ourselves as well. The most pressing issue is that of changes in our communication patterns from argument to visual image, from explanation to impression. This change in our society has been well analysed by Neil Postman in *Amusing Ourselves to Death*.[21] He comments on the great shift from the 'Age of Exposition' (marked by the printing-press) to the 'Age of Showbusiness' (marked by television). By 'exposition' he means 'a sophisticated ability to think conceptually, deductively and sequentially; a high valuation on reason and order; and abhorrence of contradiction; a large capacity for detachment and objectivity; and a tolerance for delayed response'.[22] There is of course a link between the demise of the 'Age of Exposition' and the loss of expository preaching. The same change has occurred within Christianity, and has been described by Jacques Ellul in *The Humiliation of the Word*.[23]

Is it still possible to preach, or should we hand over to pictures, sculptures, drama and dance? And if we do preach, should we persist with expository sermons? Here are some responses.

If we live in an age in which the personal presentation and declaration of truth have all but disappeared, we preachers may at least have the benefit of surprise! If our style of communication is unusual, it may well arouse interest.

Although I have linked Postman's concept of exposition with the preaching of the Bible, the two are not linked inextricably. It is *possible* to teach the Bible in the way described by Postman, and it was done in the eighteenth century. But the Evangelical Revival preached the Bible in a different way – more emotional, more demanding, calling for an immediate response. Today is not the day for a dry analysis of the Bible, but for ensuring that people meet God in his Word.

If it is suggested that we give up preaching because ordinary people cannot cope with words or the Bible, then we need to keep in mind the last time this move was made. In the seventh to the twelfth centuries, the church decided that while educated people could understand words and theology, uneducated people could best be taught through statues, stained-glass windows and pictures.[24] In many European church buildings we see evidence of this attempt at teaching the uneducated. As the Reformers discovered, it failed; it produced people who knew the gospel stories, but did not know the gospel; people who knew what had happened, but who did not know the meaning of it. A picture is not 'worth a thousand words', because it cannot teach theology.

Preaching is the God-given way of communication. God has not preserved for us a picture or audiovisual record of the crucifixion, but the

Bible describes and explains what happened. In the Bible we discover that the physical details of the crucifixion are of little importance; what it means is what matters. And that can be conveyed by preaching. Paul thus says to the Galatians: 'It was before your eyes that Jesus Christ was publicly exhibited as crucified!' (Gal. 3:1).

Our preaching does not have to be as unemotional, dry, unimaginative and uninvolving as we can make it. For some curious reason, we assume that 'intellectual' means 'unemotional', and 'emotional' means 'un-intellectual'. But the Bible shows us that truth can be passionate. And if God has spoken this way, we ought to do the same. As Martyn Lloyd-Jones says, 'What is preaching? Logic on fire!'[25]

Though I think we ought to go on preaching expository sermons, we must be compassionate towards our hearers, and teach them gently how to listen. At one congregation where I worked, the prescribed sermon limit was eleven minutes when I arrived. Six years later I had edged them up to accept twenty-eight minutes – and even the choir stayed awake. My point is that we should be aware of our congregation and the particular features of twentieth-century life that its members share – not that we should be controlled by them, but that we should interact with them compassion-ately. It is not their fault that they live in the twentieth century!

We can of course supplement our monologue with some dialogue, since the monologue form is not God-given. One option would be to preach for twenty minutes and then discuss or answer questions for twenty minutes. Both would be 'the explanation and application of the Word'.

The other issues that people come up against have to do not with hearing a sermon but with relating it to their everyday lives. People in our congregations are overworked or unemployed, they confront tough moral issues at work or at home or with their friends, they feel increasingly marginalized and weak in the face of many different kinds of problems around the world, they find it increasingly difficult to do anything about the bad news that they hear from the media every day, and they have to cope with severe personal, emotional and family crises. I list these problems not to discourage us but to remind us of the real state of the people to whom we preach. Our preaching must be based on compassion for them and knowledge of them, just as Jesus' preaching was based on compassion for those who were 'harassed and helpless, like sheep without a shepherd' (Mt. 9:36). Gabriel Hebert comments:

> The Sermon is an important element in the liturgy: its function is to save the liturgy from the danger of becoming formalistic. It is the prophetic declaration that the faith which is enshrined in the forms of worship is the living faith of those here present. Such preaching will be 'theological' in the true sense. It will deal with God, with God's work of grace, and man's

reconciliation with God . . . It will connect the liturgy with private prayer, by bringing the unchanging forms of the service into relation with the 'here' and 'now'. For every sermon that is a good sermon is, so to speak, dated and addressed.[26]

Suffering

For Paul, Christian ministry is inescapably linked with suffering. 'I think that God exhibited us apostles as last of all, as though sentenced to death, because we have become a spectacle to the world, to angels and to mortals . . . We have become like the rubbish of the world, the dregs of all things' (1 Cor. 4:9, 11–13). 'We have this treasure in clay jars, so that it may be made clear that this extraordinary power belongs to God and does not come from us . . . always carrying in the body the death of Jesus, so that the life of Jesus may also be made visible in our bodies' (2 Cor. 4:7, 10).

Paul saw suffering as an integral part of his ministry. He suffered for the benefit of those he was trying to win for Christ and to present mature in Christ.

> We are putting no obstacle in anyone's way, so that no fault will be found with our ministry, but as servants of God we have commended ourselves in every way: through great endurance; in afflictions, hardships, calamities, beatings, imprisonments, riots, labours, sleepless nights, hunger; by purity, knowledge, patience, kindness; holiness of spirit, genuine love, truthful speech, and the power of God; with the weapons of right-eousness for the right hand and for the left; in honour and dishonour, in ill repute and good repute. We are treated as impostors, and yet are true; as unknown, and yet are well known; as dying, and see – we are alive; as punished, and yet not killed; as sorrowful, yet always rejoicing; as poor, yet making many rich; as having nothing, and yet possessing everything.
>
> We have spoken frankly to you Corinthians; our heart is wide open to you . . . open wide your hearts also. (2 Cor. 6:3–13; see also 11:21–29)

For most of us at the present time, our suffering does not take dramatic forms. But it would be hard to imagine that we could engage in the kind of ministry that Paul describes without some kind of suffering. Suffering is probably most often experienced as stress and frustration in our lives and ministries. This stress is caused by the magnitude of the job we have to do, our high expectation of God's work in the world, our frustration with ourselves and our weakness and sinfulness, and with our people, our disappointments in ministry, and the apparent lack of progress of the gospel all around us. These stresses and frustrations will inevitably mean that in some sense we suffer because of the ministry in which we engage.

For some of us at the present time, and perhaps for more of us in the future, suffering will also involve real dispute, hardship and heartache as we make a stand for gospel truth and gospel ministry and are persecuted by either the church or the world. Christian martyrdom has certainly been on the agenda for the world in the twentieth century. There is no reason to think that the twenty-first will be any easier.

So far we have been describing preaching as a demanding ministry: demanding because it involves so much of our life and so much of our energy. It demands love and obedience to God and Christ, commitment to the truth of God, love for people, hard work, relating to the real world in which people live, suffering, and a life of ministry.

Our sufficiency is from God

In relation to new-covenant ministry Paul asks: 'Who is sufficient for these things?' (2 Cor. 2:16). The answer that he himself gives is that 'our competence [our sufficiency, our ability] is from God, who has made us competent [sufficient] to be ministers of a new covenant' (3:5–6). This treasure is in clay jars, to make clear God's extraordinary power in our ministries (2 Cor. 4:7). It is important to see that the things for which God makes Paul sufficient include not just his grasp of the gospel, but also his use of his intellect and emotions, and his whole life, in the service of the gospel.

The Westminster Larger Catechism provides a fine summary of the demands of the preaching ministry in the context of the God who calls and enables.

> Question: How is the word of God to be preached by those that are called thereunto?
>
> Answer: They that are called to labour in the ministry of the word are to preach sound doctrine, diligently, in season and out of season; plainly, not in the enticing words of man's wisdom, but in demonstration of the Spirit, and of power; faithfully, making known the whole counsel of God; wisely, applying themselves to the necessities and capacities of the hearers; zealously, with fervent love to God and the souls of his people; sincerely, aiming at his glory, and their conversion, edification, and salvation.[27]

If preaching is demanding for the preacher, it should also be demanding for the hearers. Again the summary in the Westminster Larger Catechism is useful.

Question: What is required of those who hear the word preached?

Answer: It is required of those that hear the word preached that they attend upon it with diligence, preparation and prayer; examine what they hear by the scriptures; receive the truth with faith, love, meekness, and readiness of mind, as the word of God; meditate, and confer on it; hide it in their hearts, and bring forth the fruit of it in their lives.[28]

Conclusion

I have tried to provide a robust and practical theology of preaching. In Part 1 we studied the theological foundations of preaching, which lie in the convictions that *God has spoken*, that he has preserved his words for future generations (*It is written*), and that he calls people to be ministers of his Word (*Preach the Word*). In Part Two we looked at the variety of ways in which the Word of God is ministered in our congregations, and clarified the special features of preaching, which I defined as 'the explanation and application of the Word to the congregation in order to produce corporate preparation for service, unity of faith, maturity, growth, and upbuilding'. We also investigated New Testament evidence which helps us to understand preaching. We then studied various aspects of the preacher's Bible, and noted how a good and realistic theology of the Bible will help us in shaping our preaching. Next we analysed the preacher's purpose: to serve God, the text and the people of God, and we saw how these priorities were exemplified in the theology and practice of John Calvin. Finally we looked at preaching as a demanding ministry. My aim has been to discover, explain and commend what the Bible teaches about preaching as a ministry of the Word.

We conclude with the text from which the title of this book is taken, with its great encouragement to all ministers of the Word:

Whoever speaks must do so as one *speaking the very words of God* . . . so that God may be glorified in all things through Jesus Christ. (1 Pet. 4:11)

Notes

1. John R. W. Stott, *I Believe in Preaching* (London: Hodder and Stoughton, 1982), p. 82.

2. The following quotations are from *The Works of John Owen*, vol. 4, ed. W. H. Goold (Edinburgh: Banner of Truth, 1967).

3. *Ibid.*, p. 509.

4. *Ibid.*, p. 510.

5. *Ibid.*, pp. 510–511.

6. *Ibid.*, pp. 512–513.

7. *Ibid.*, p. 482.

8. Stott, *I Believe in Preaching*, pp. 334–335.

9. Calvin on Je. 3:4, quoted in Miller, *Calvin's Wisdom*, p. 252.

10. John MacArthur Jr, *Rediscovering Expository Preaching* (Waco: Word, 1992), p. 348. I am grateful to my colleague Ivan Lee for this reference.

11. John Killinger, *Fundamentals of Preaching* (London: SCM, 1985), front cover.

12. Stott, *I Believe in Preaching*, p. 191.

13. D. Martyn Lloyd-Jones, *Preaching and Preachers* (London: Hodder and Stoughton, 1985), p. 92.

14. Charles Simeon, quoted in Charles Smyth, *The Art of Preaching, 747–1939* (London: SPCK, 1940), p. 177.

15. Leander Keck, *The Bible in the Pulpit* (Nashville: Abingdon, 1978), p. 120.

16. *The Directory for the Public Worship of God*, pp. 380–381.

17. *Ibid.*, p. 381.

18. John Stott, in his Editor's Introduction to *Evangelical Preaching: An Anthology of Sermons by Charles Simeon* (Portland: Multnomah, 1986), p. xxxvii.

19. R. E. C. Browne, *The Ministry of the Word* (London: SCM, 1958), p. 44.

20. Leander Keck, *The Bible in the Pulpit*, ch. 1: 'The Malaise of Biblical Preaching', pp. 11ff., Runia, *The Sermon under Attack*, ch. 1: 'Contemporary Criticisms', pp. 1ff., Stott, *I Believe in Preaching*, ch. 2: 'Contemporary Objections to Preaching', pp. 50ff., Martyn Lloyd-Jones, *Preaching and Preachers*, chs. 1–3.

21. Neil Postman, *Amusing Ourselves to Death* (London: Methuen, 1987).

22. *Ibid.*, p. 64.

23. Jacques Ellul, *The Humiliation of the Word* (Grand Rapids: Eerdmans, 1985). See also Simon Vibert, *The Church in the Age of the TV Image* (Hartford: Fellowship of Word and Spirit, 1993).

24. The idea that pictures could be the Bible of the uneducated was put forward by Pope Gregory in Epistle 9.9.

25. Lloyd-Jones, *Preaching and Preachers*, p. 97.

26. A. G. Hebert, *Liturgy and Society* (London: Faber, 1961), pp. 222–223.

27. In *The Confession of Faith and Other Documents* (London: Wickliffe Press, 1962), pp. 251–252.

28. *Ibid.*, p. 253.